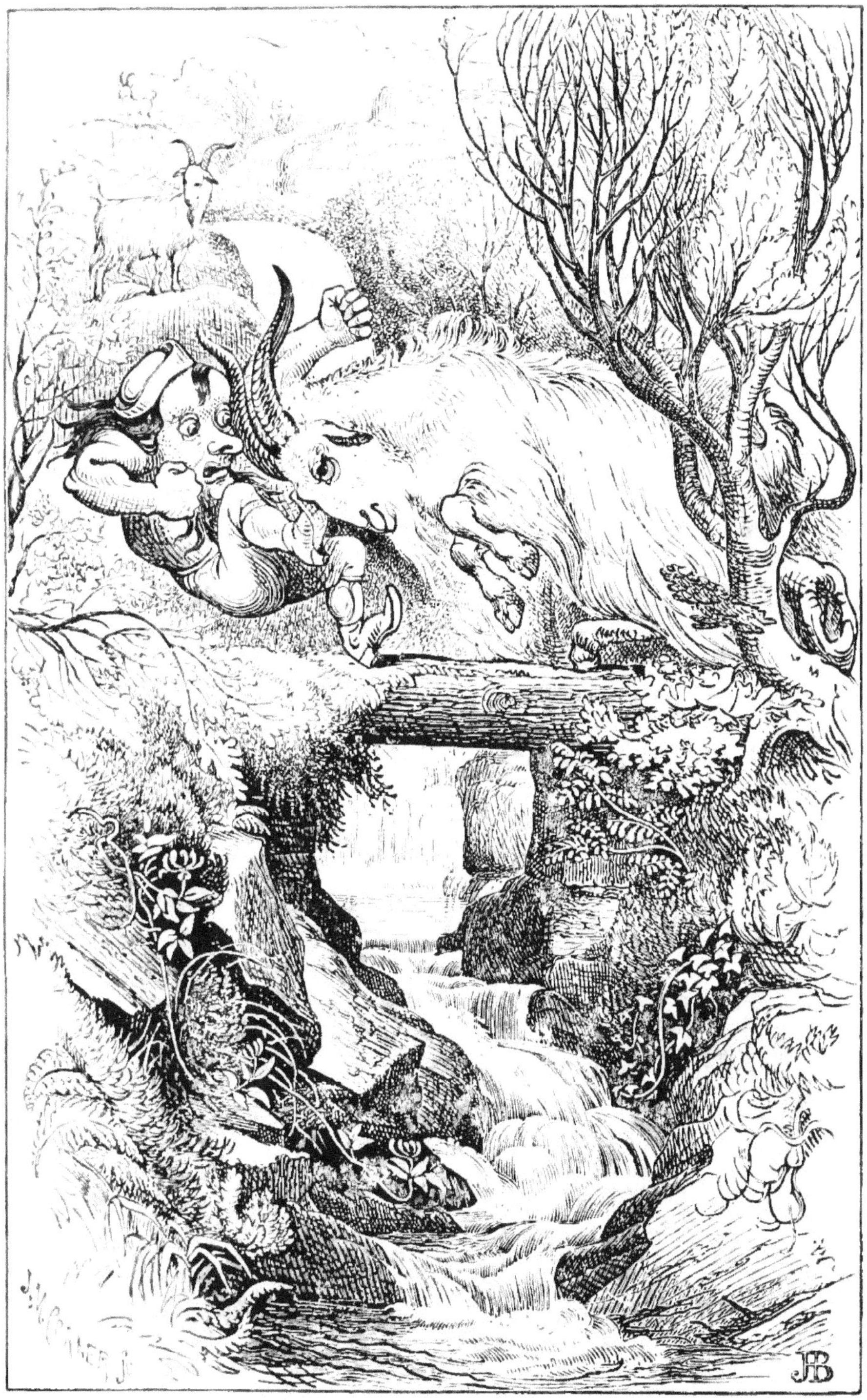

The Three Billy-Goats Gruff

(*See page 238*)

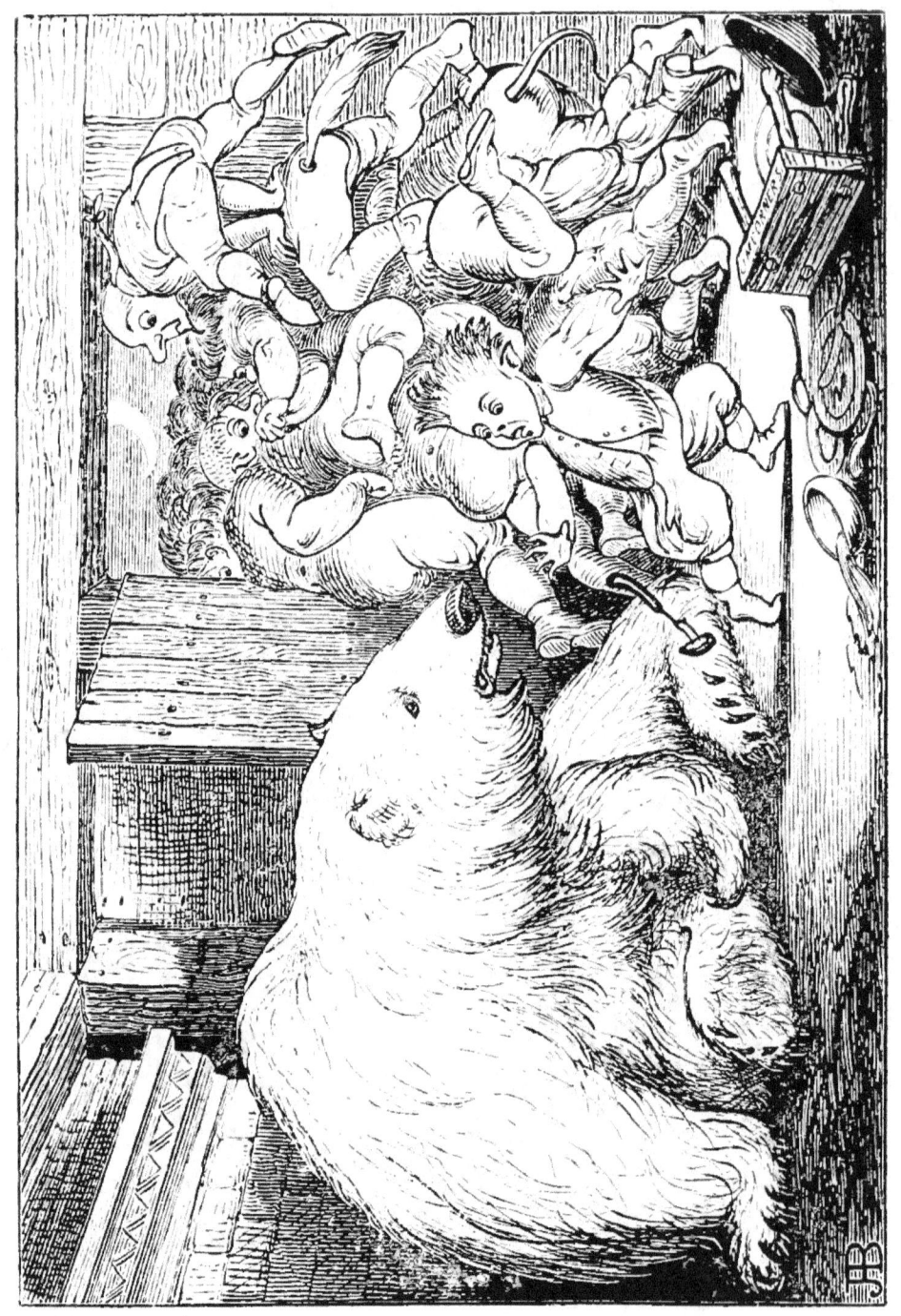

The Cat on the Dovrefell

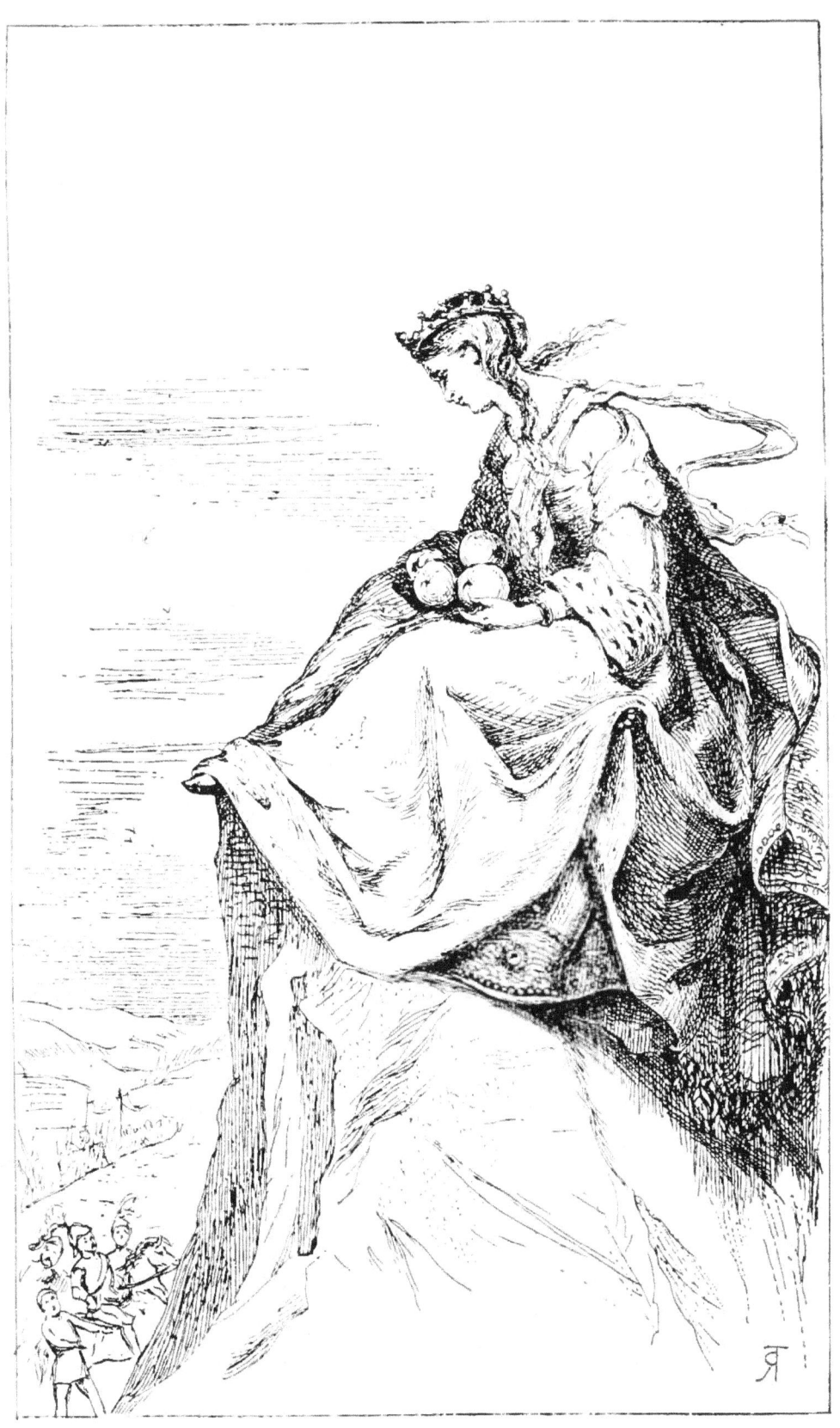

The Princess on the Glass Hill

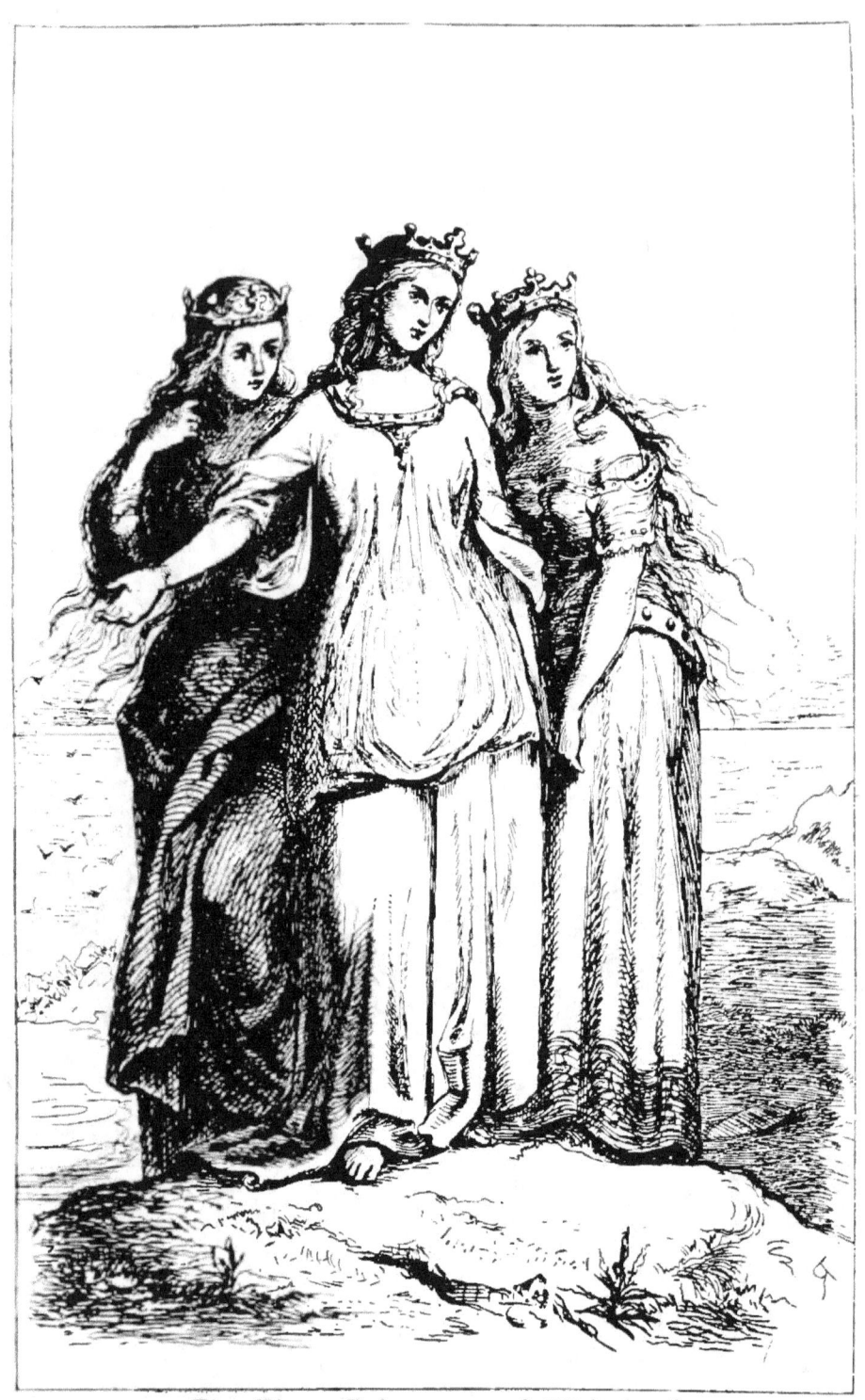
The Three Princesses of Whiteland

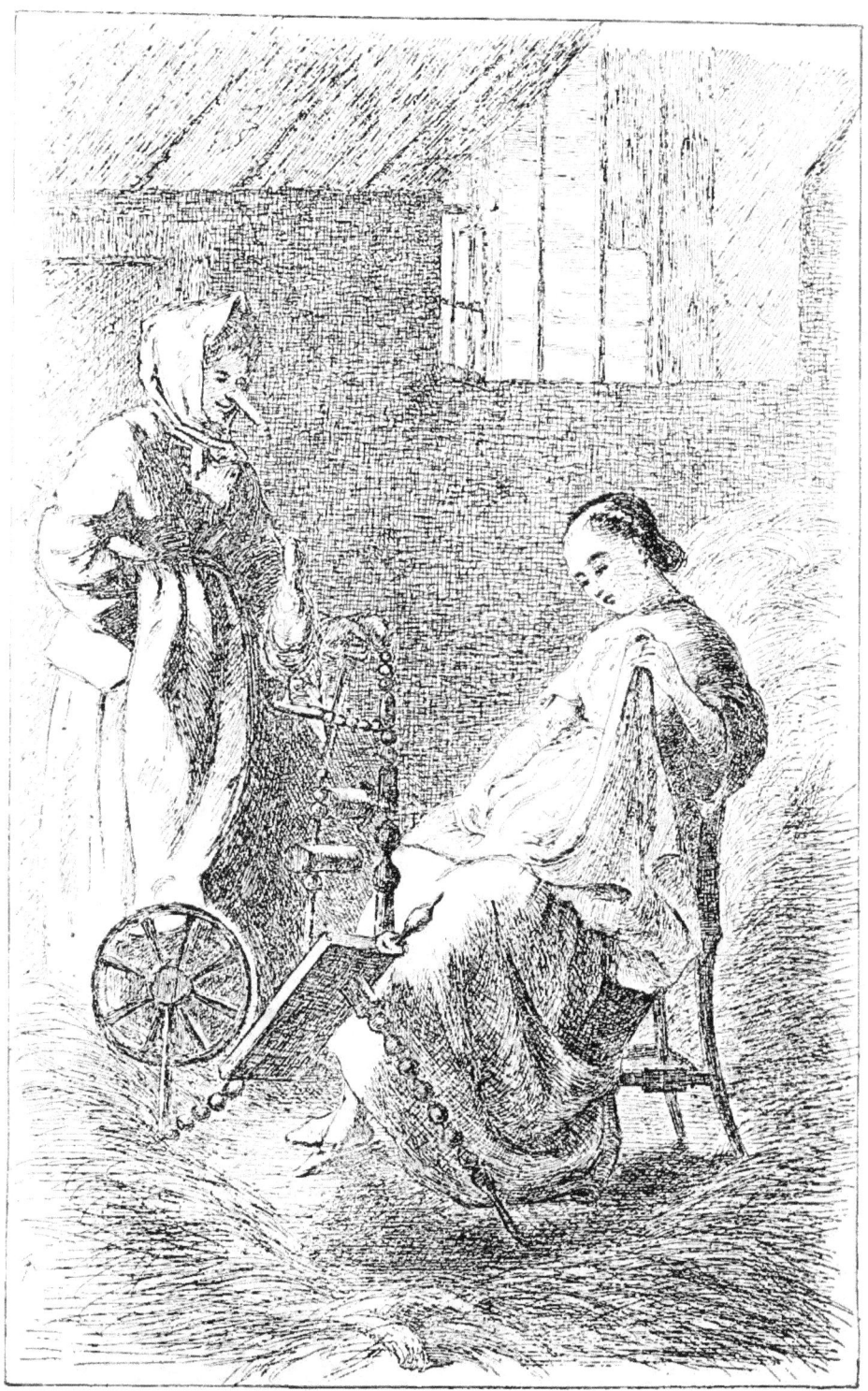

The Three Aunts

Rich Peter the Pedlar

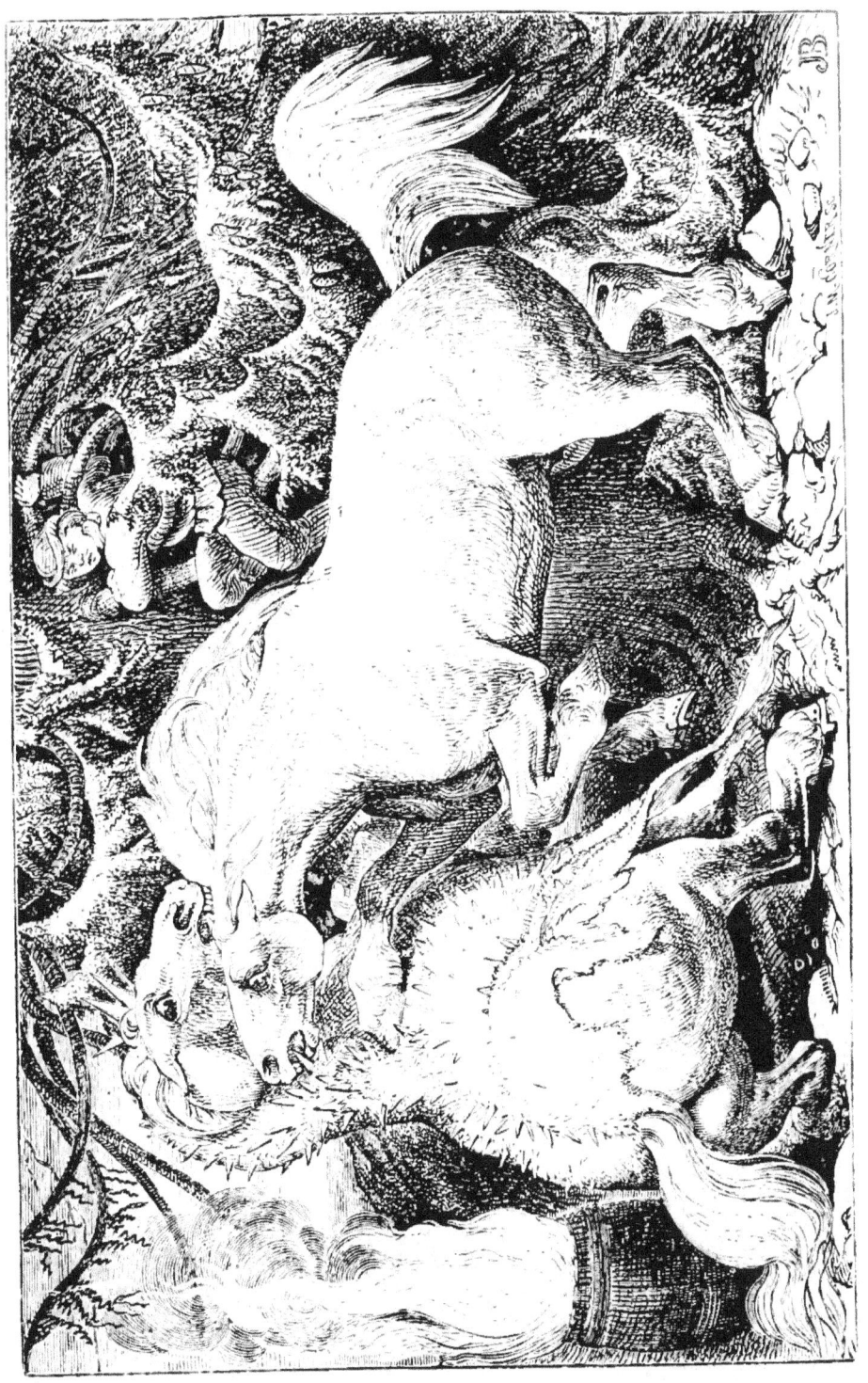

Dapplegrim

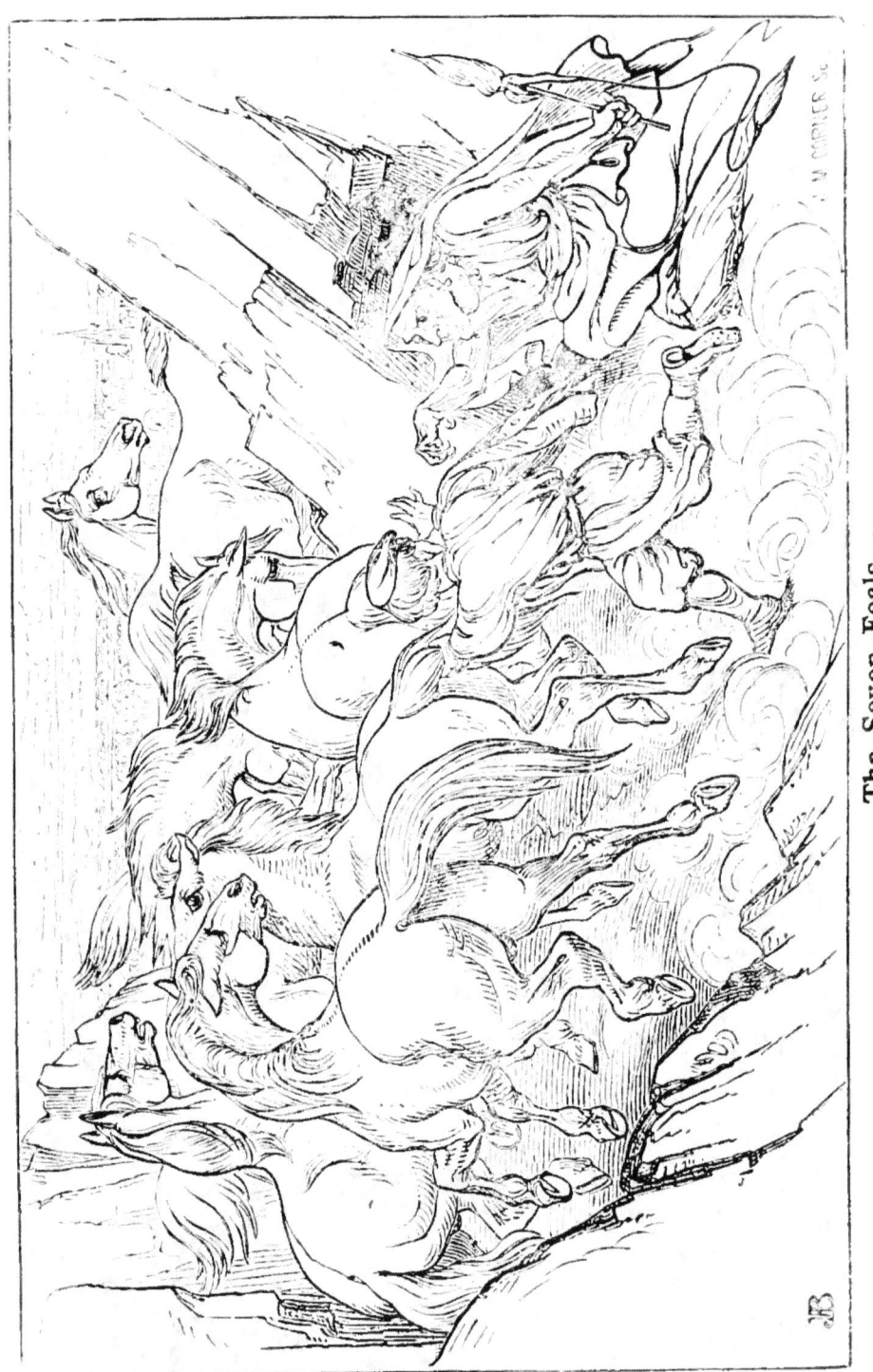

The Seven Foals

Kay Nielsen

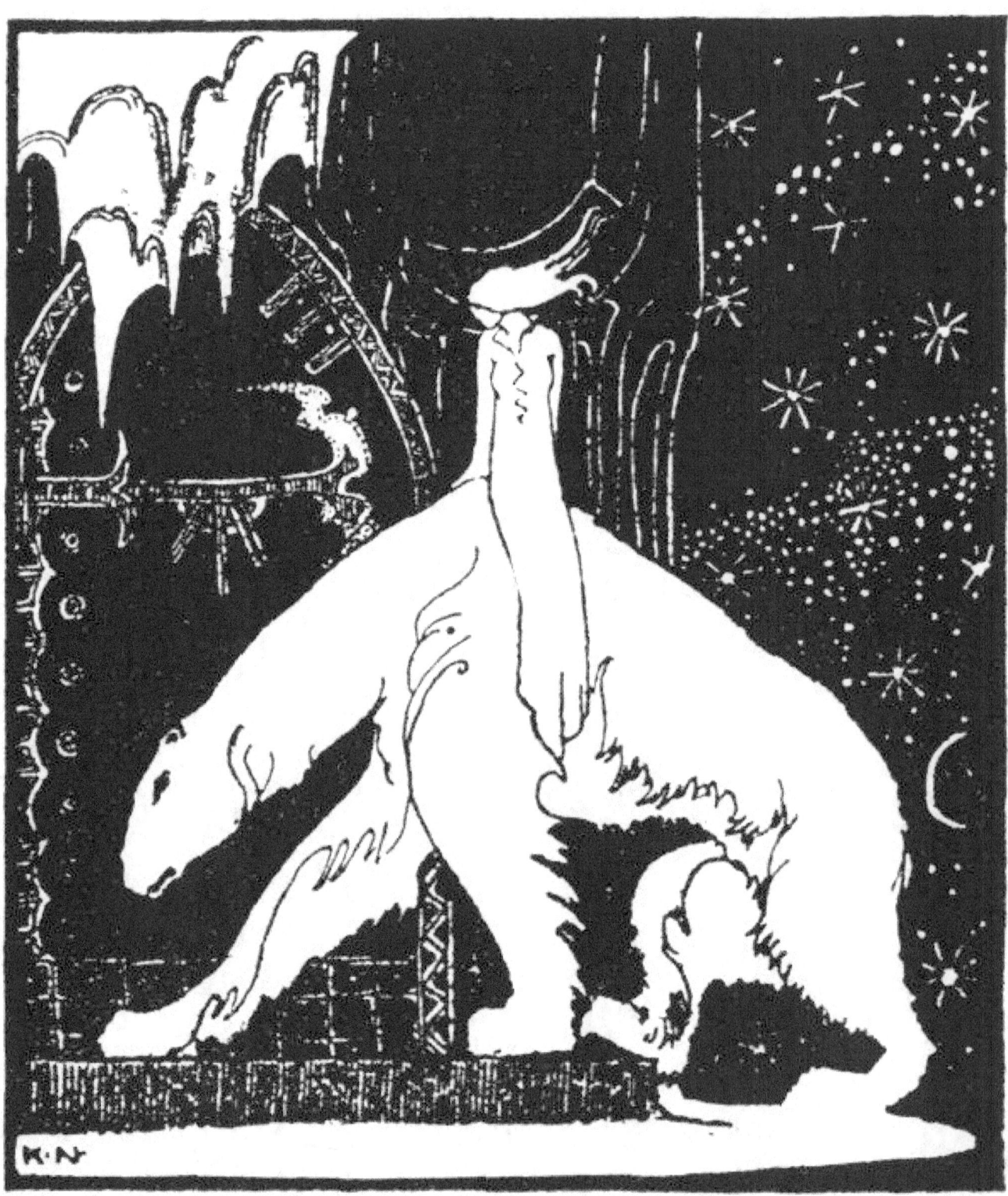

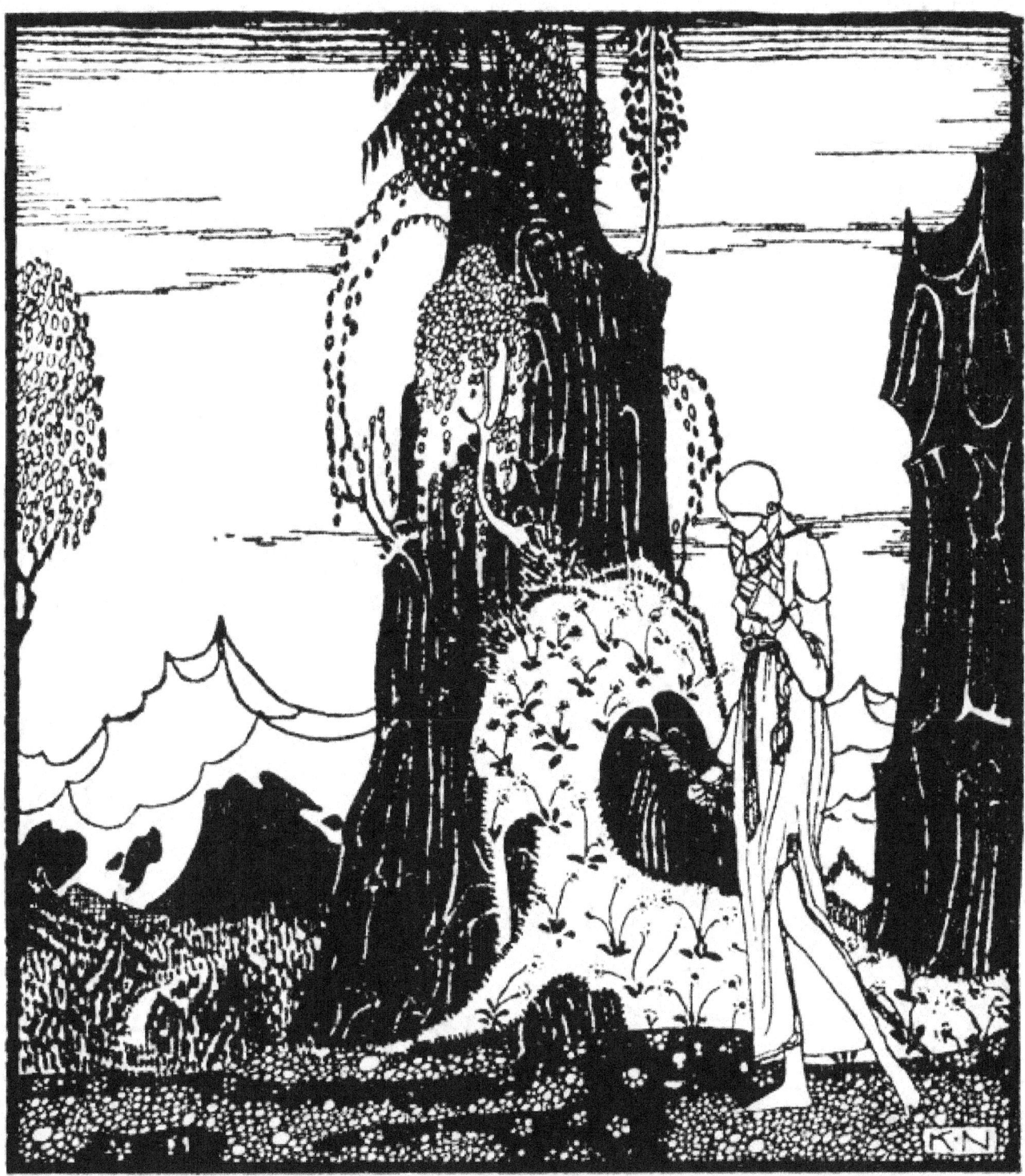

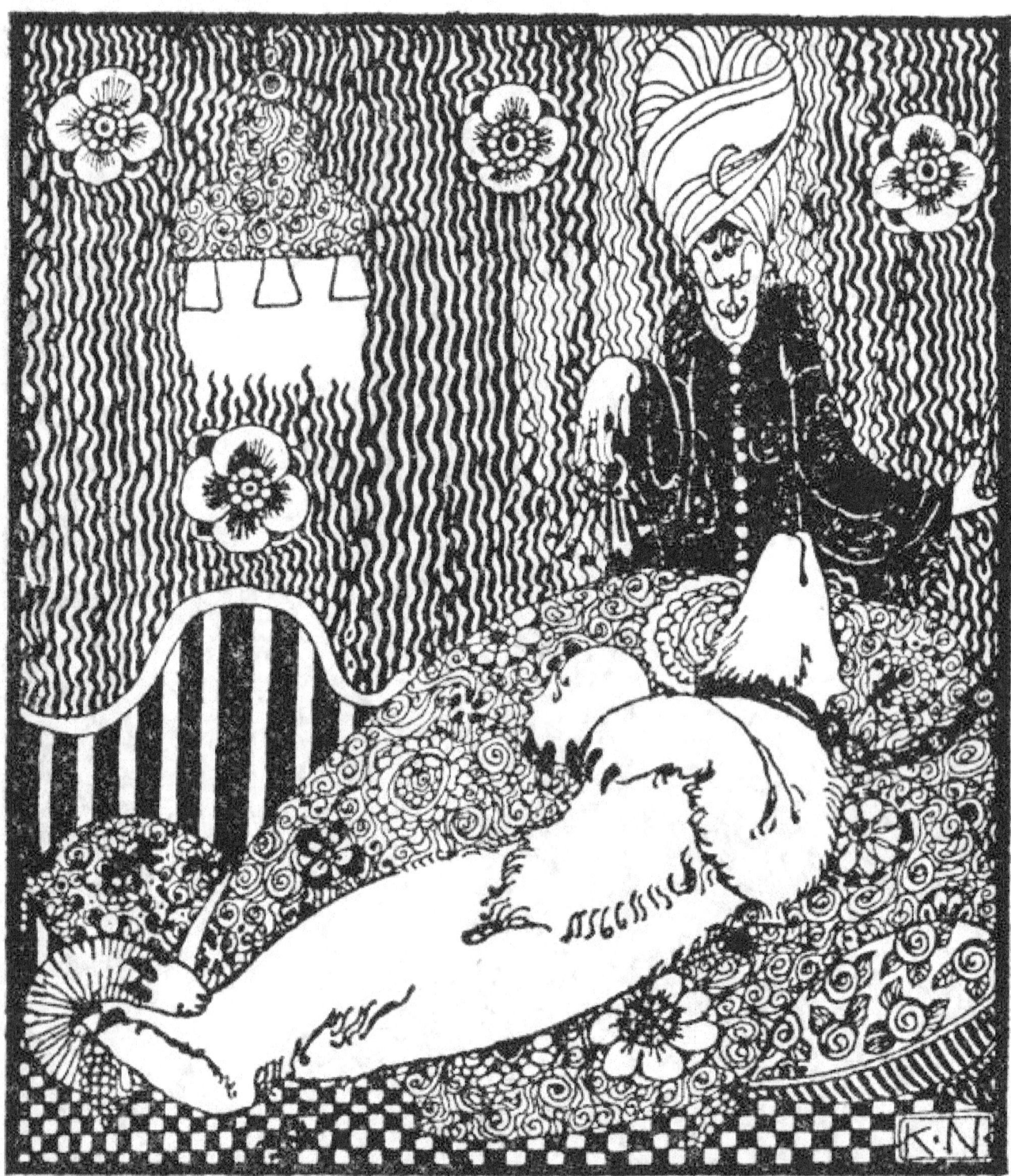

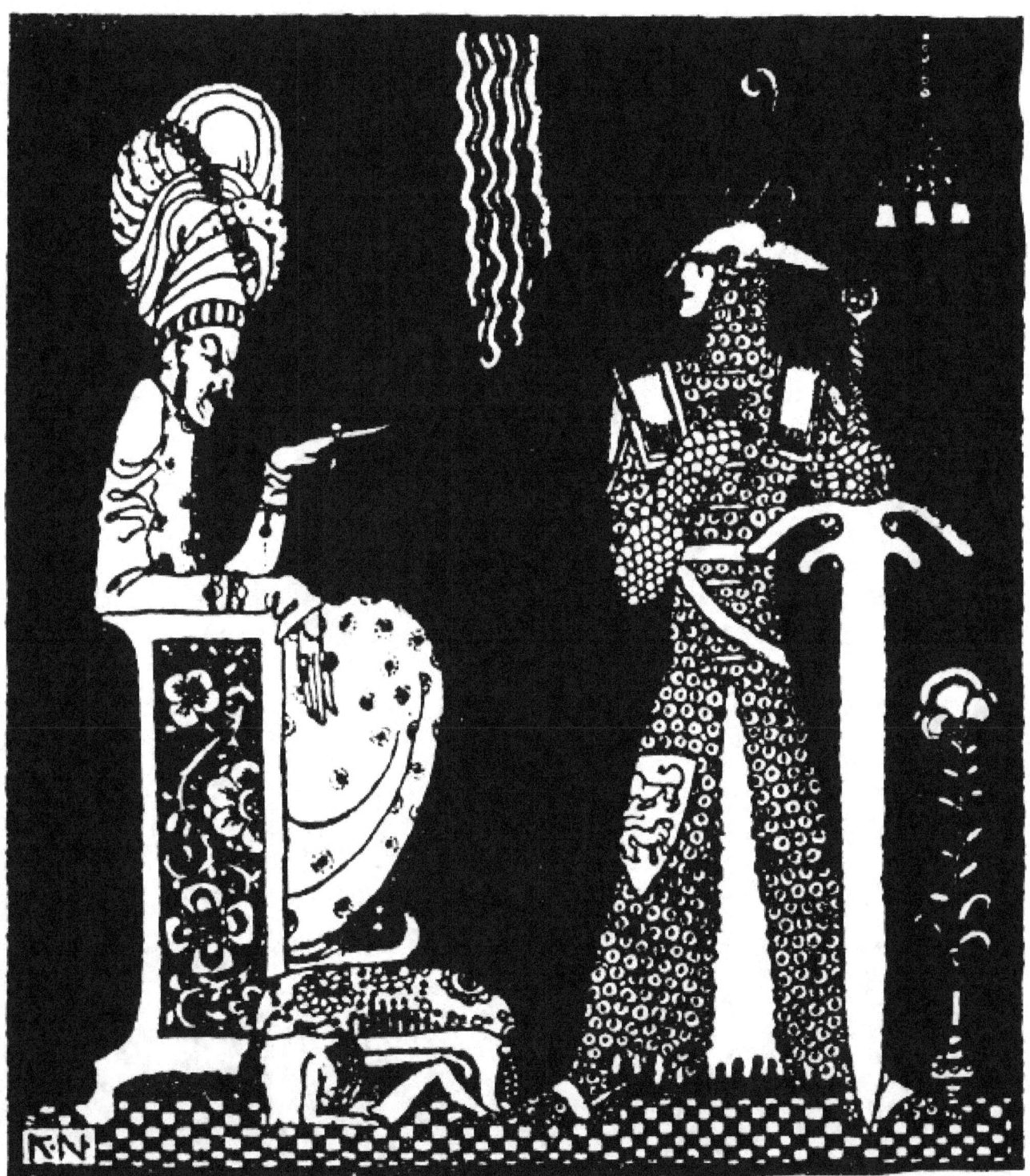

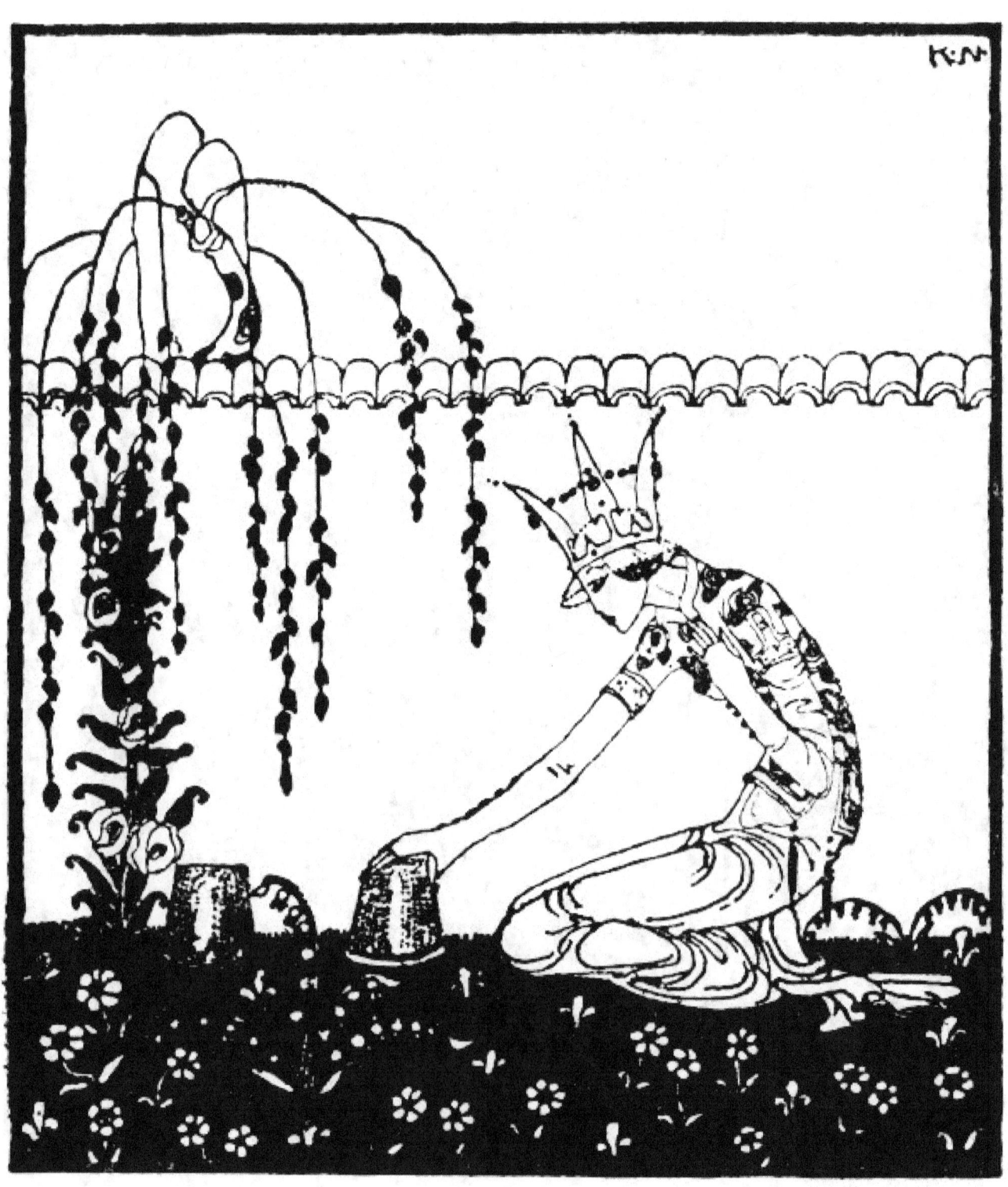

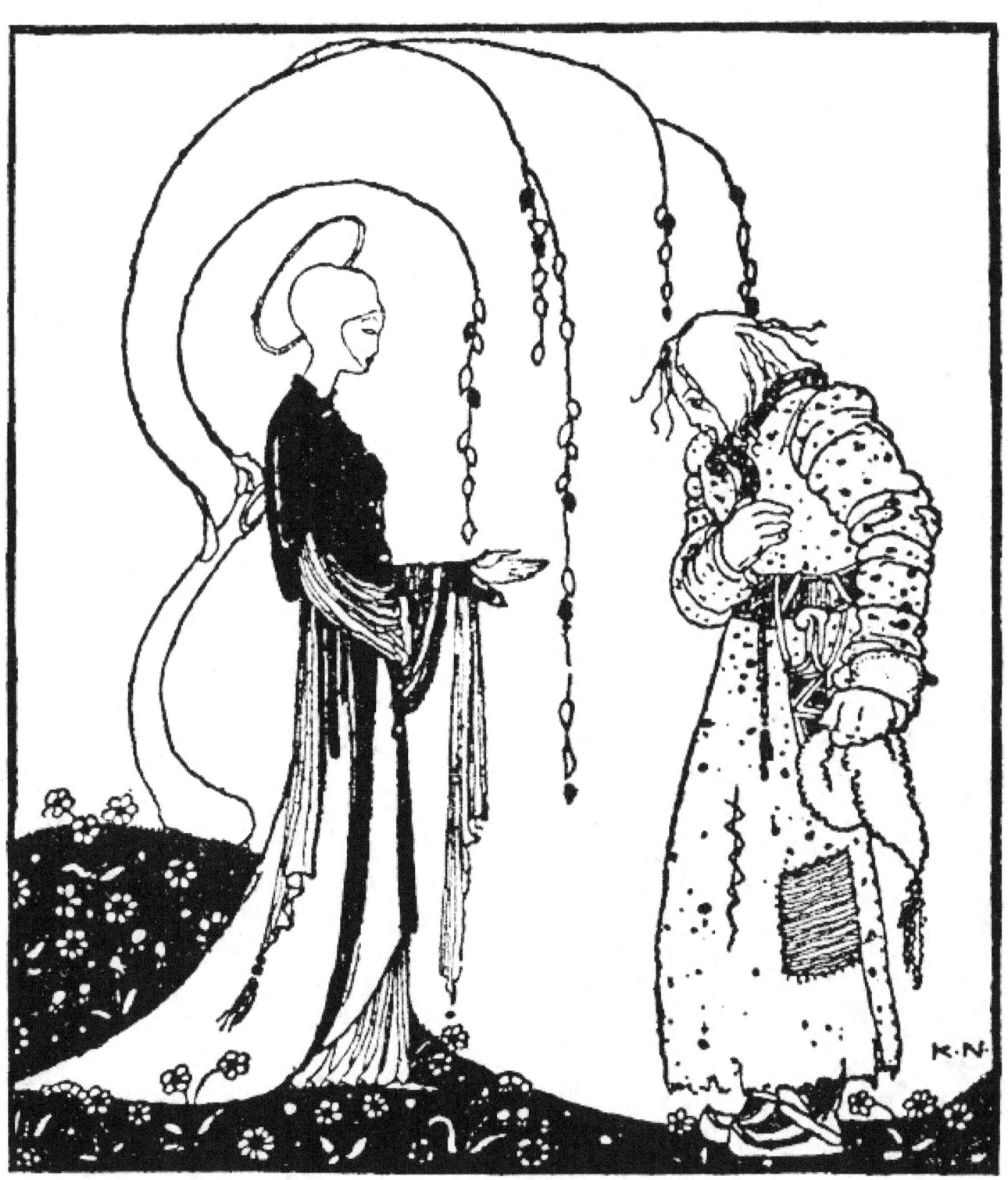

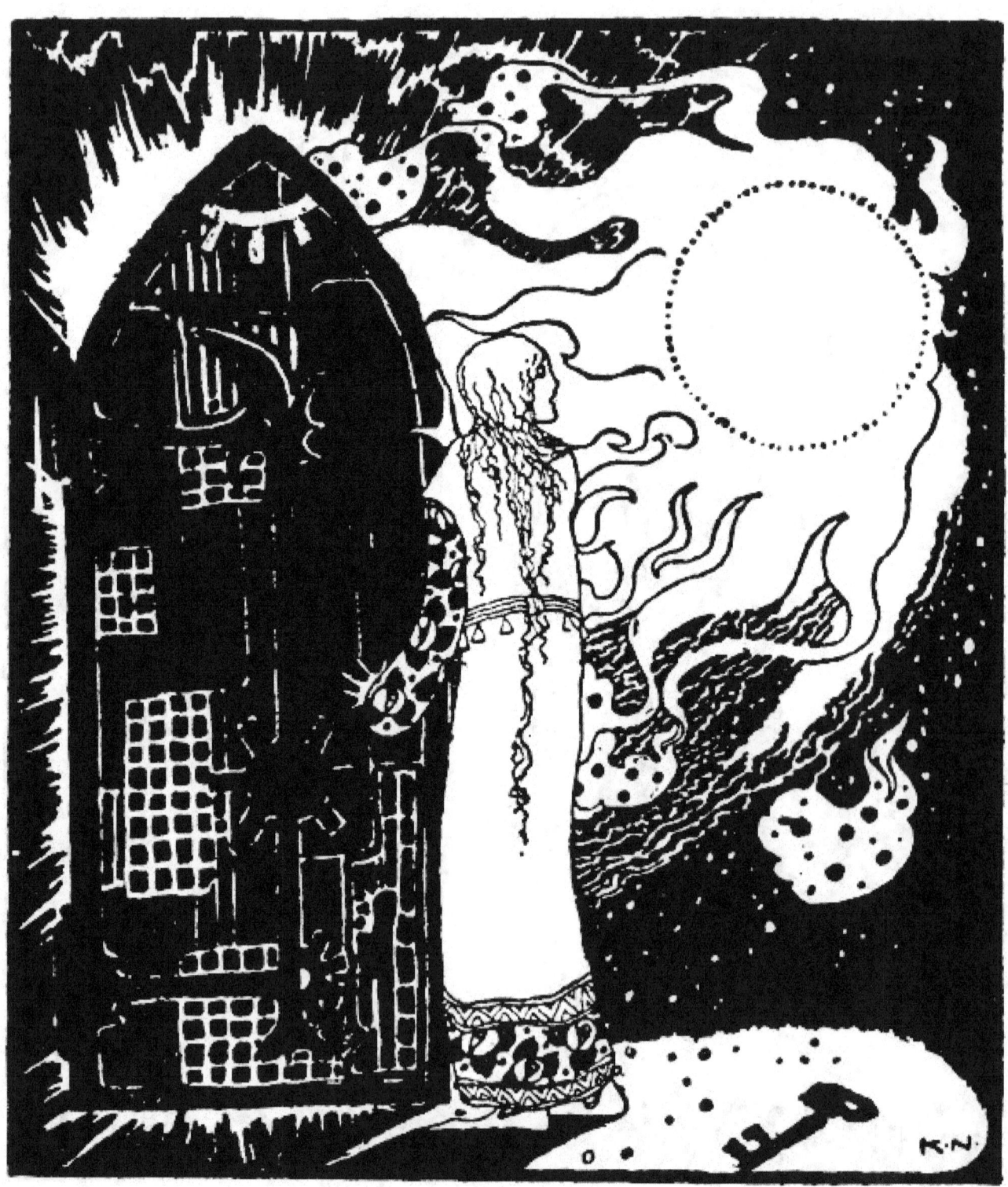

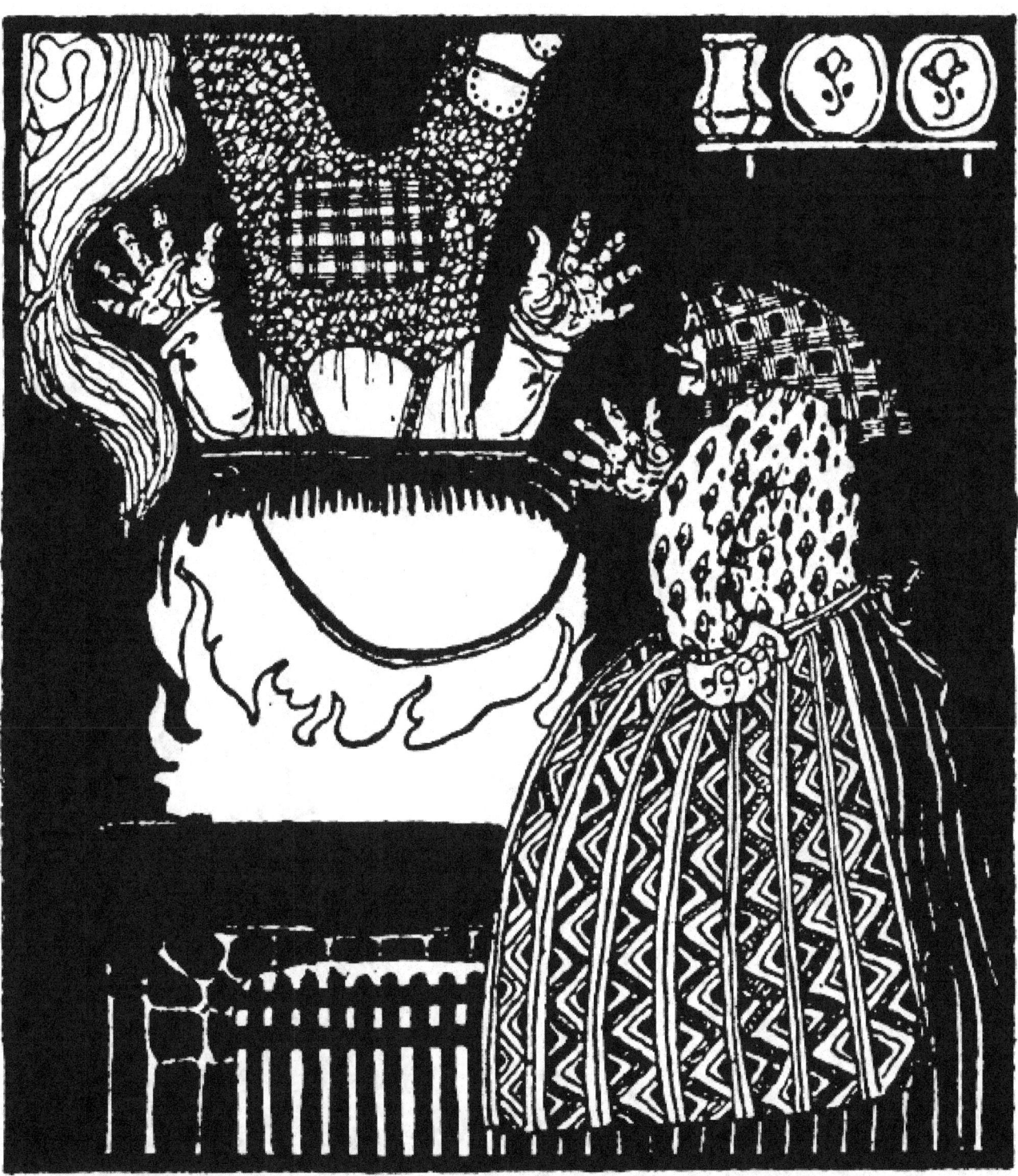

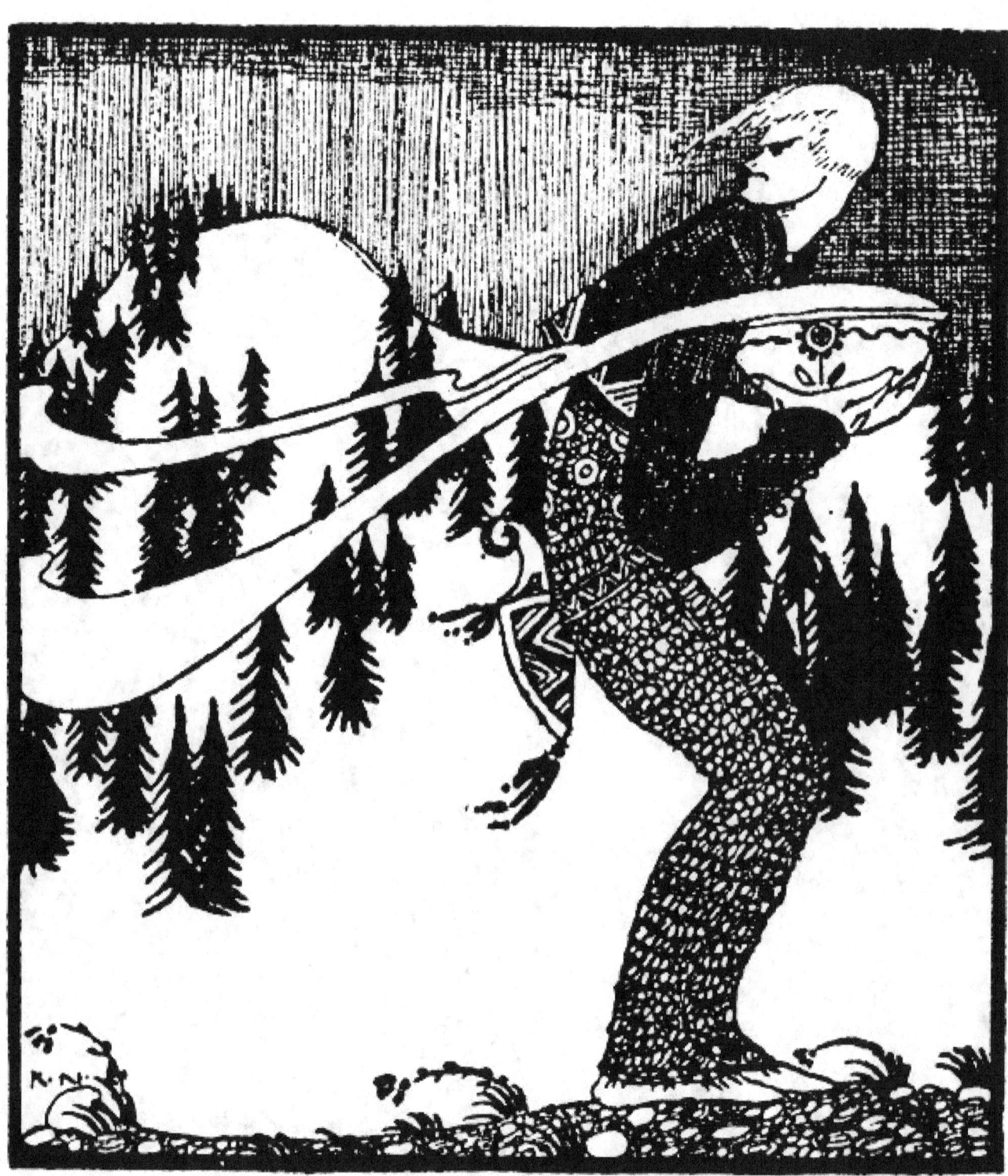

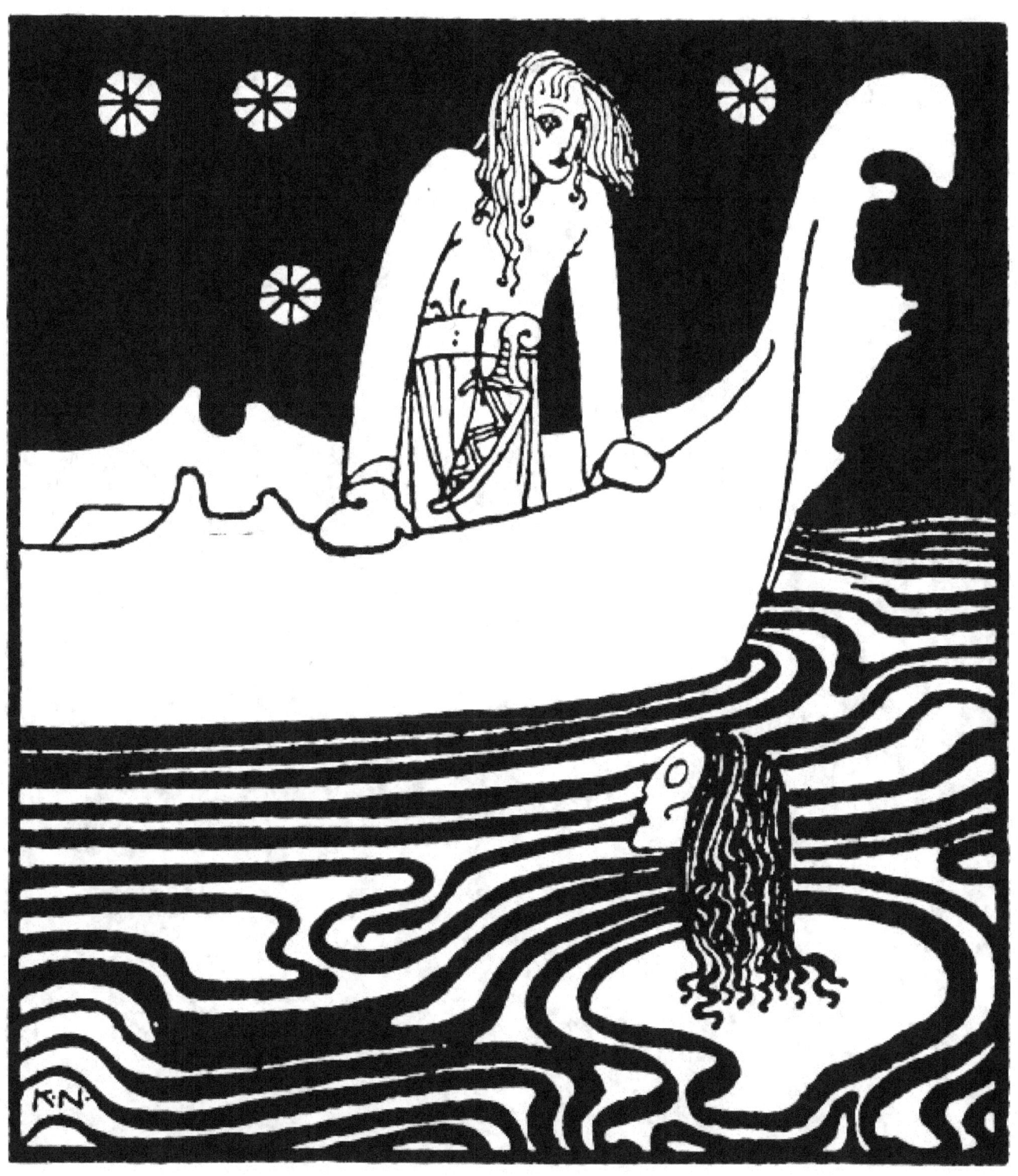

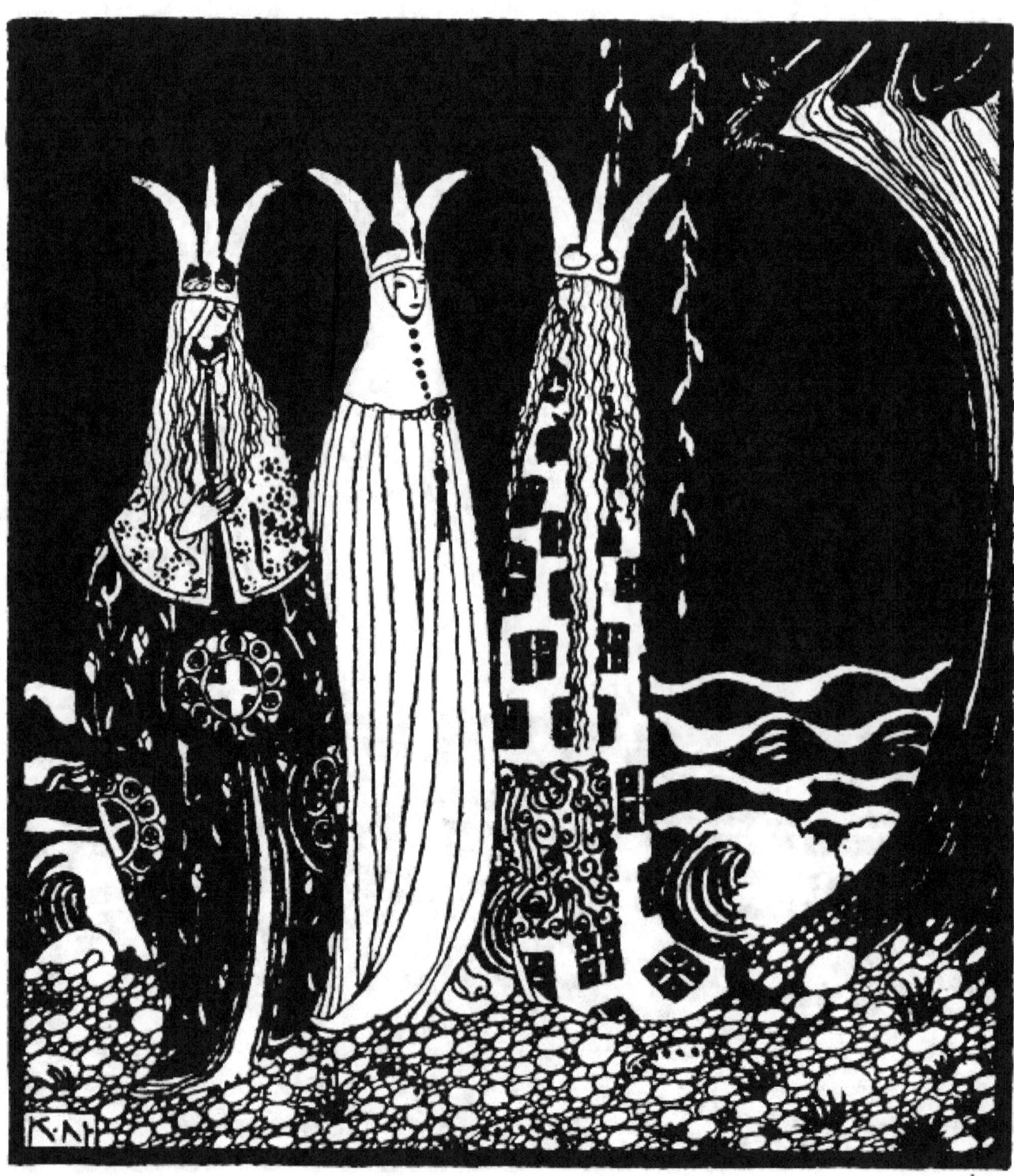

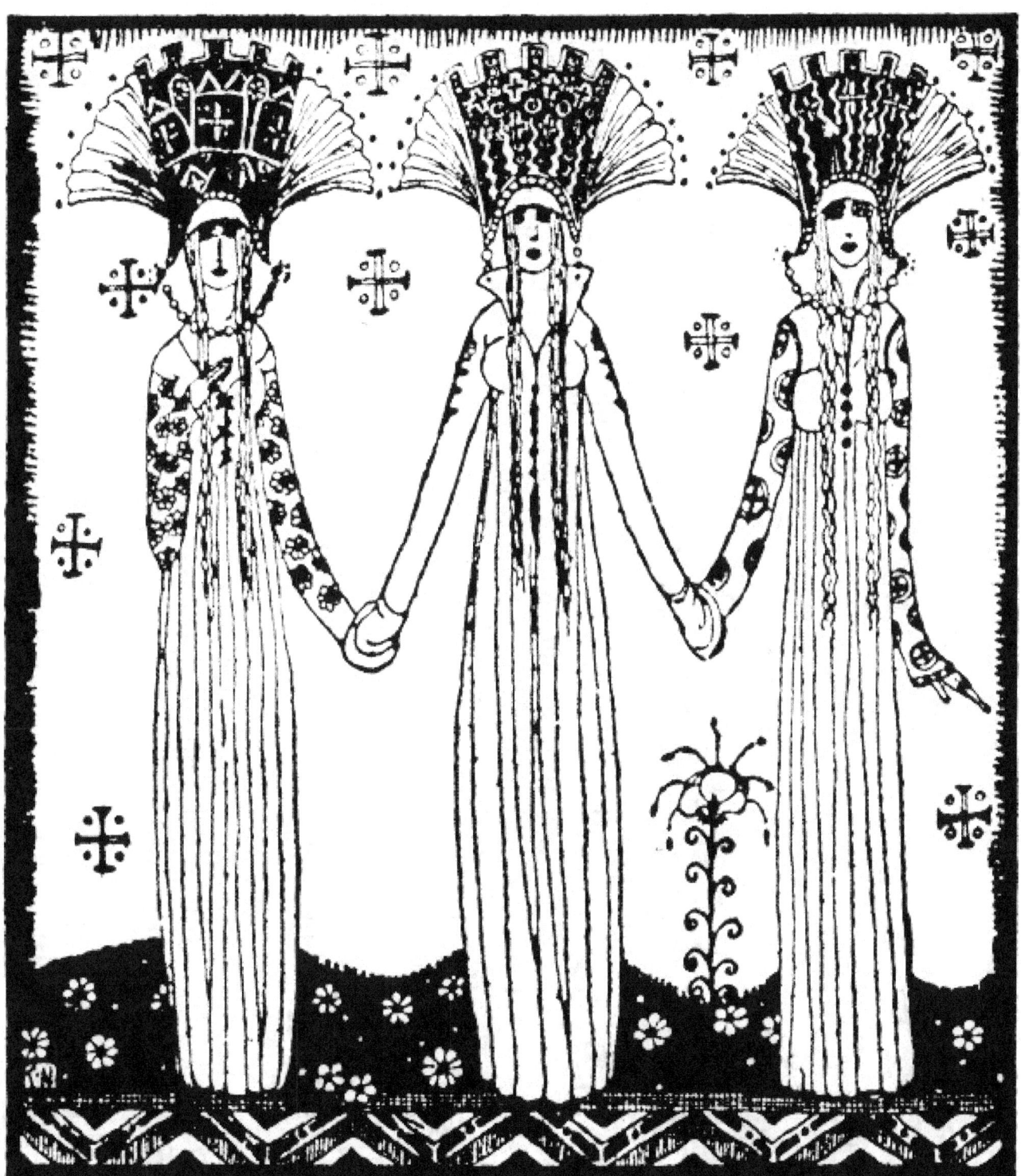

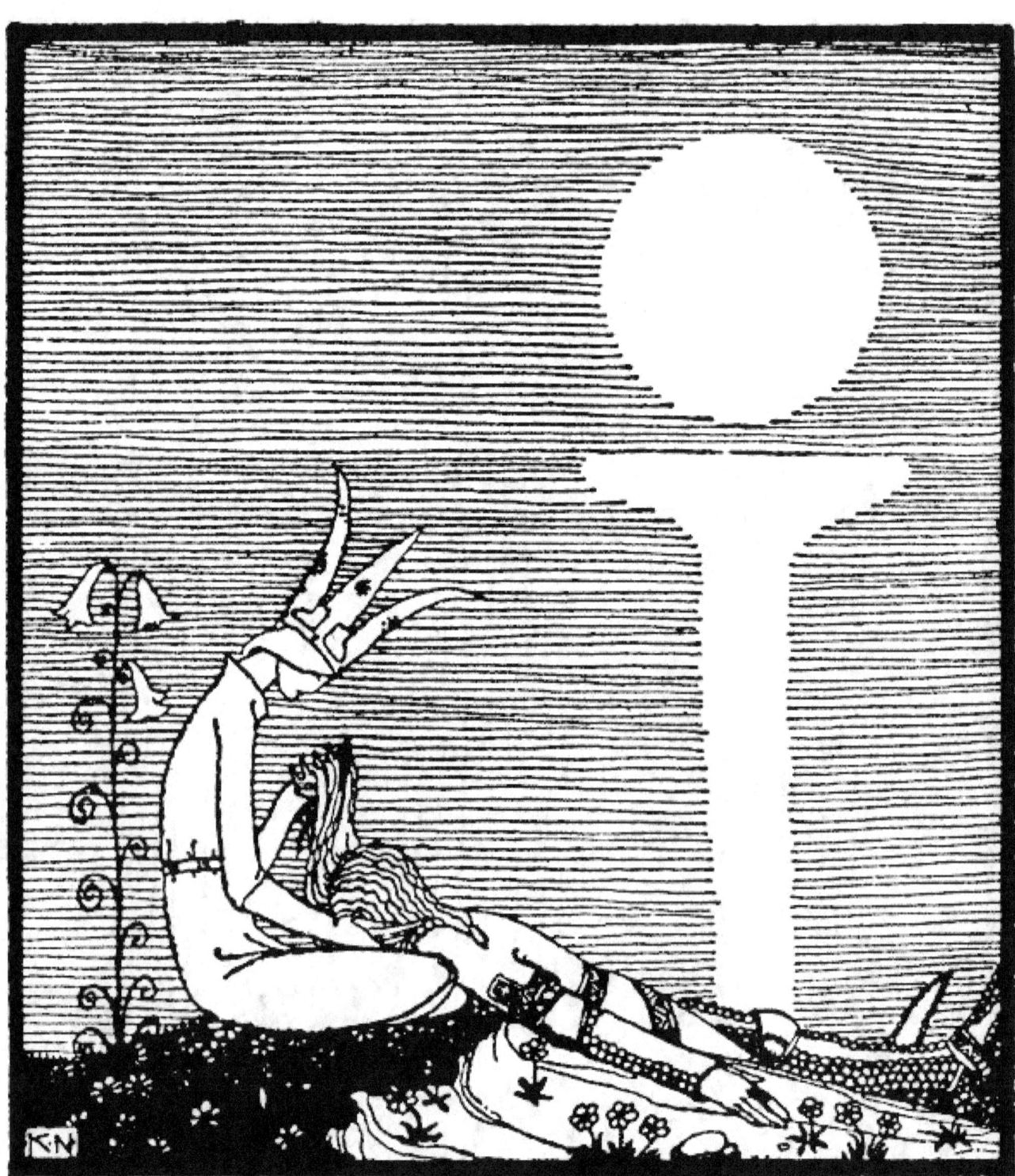

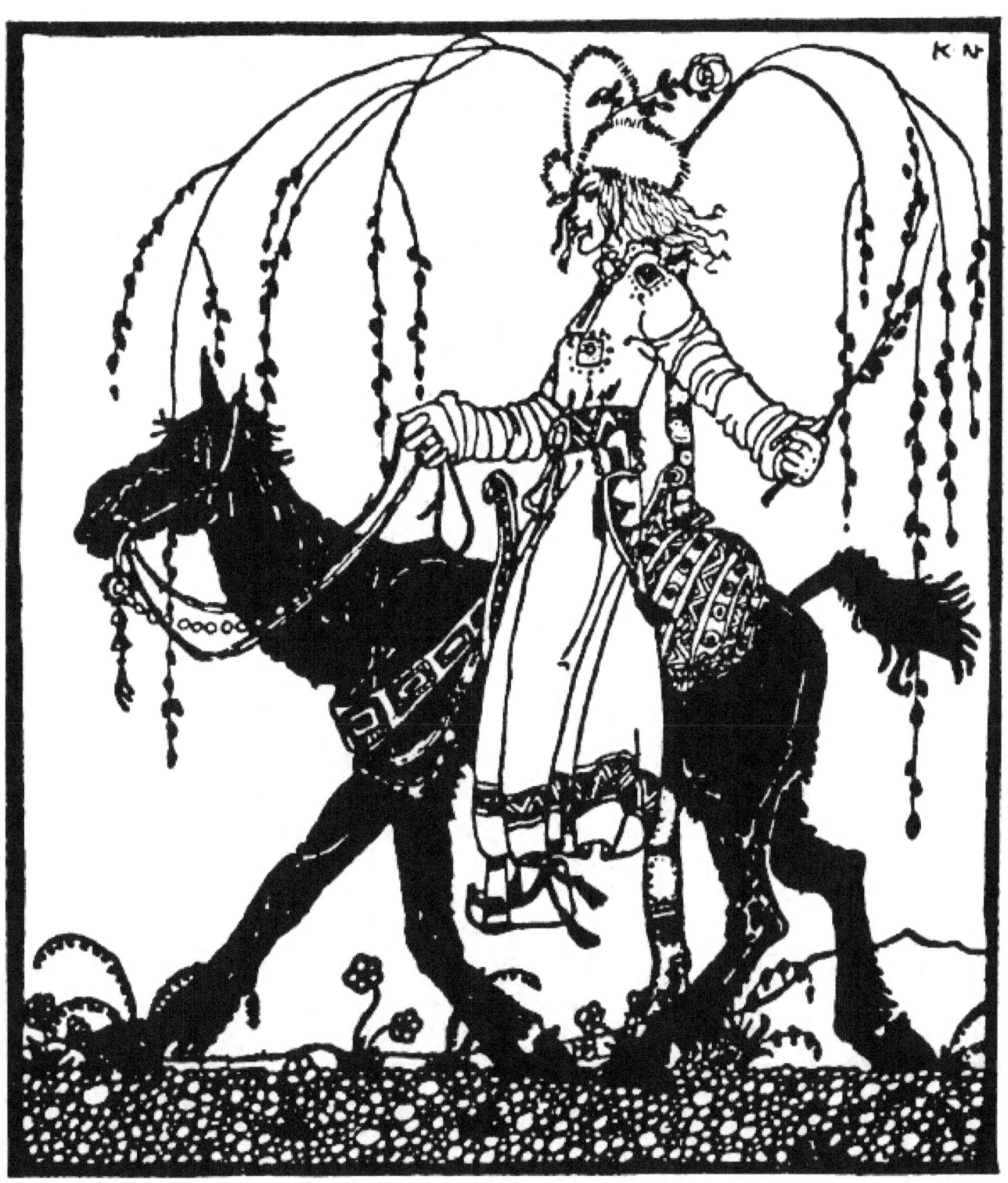

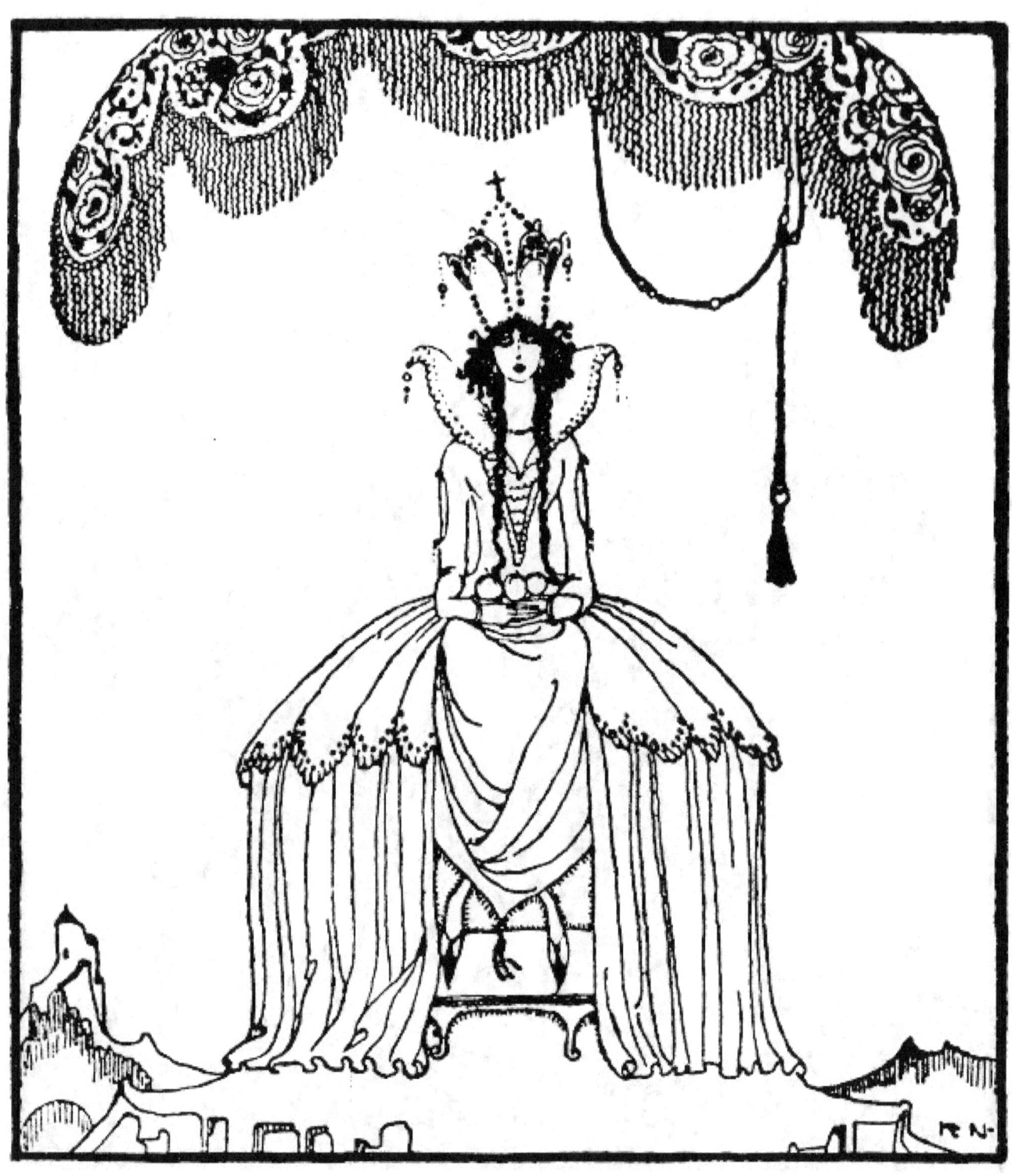

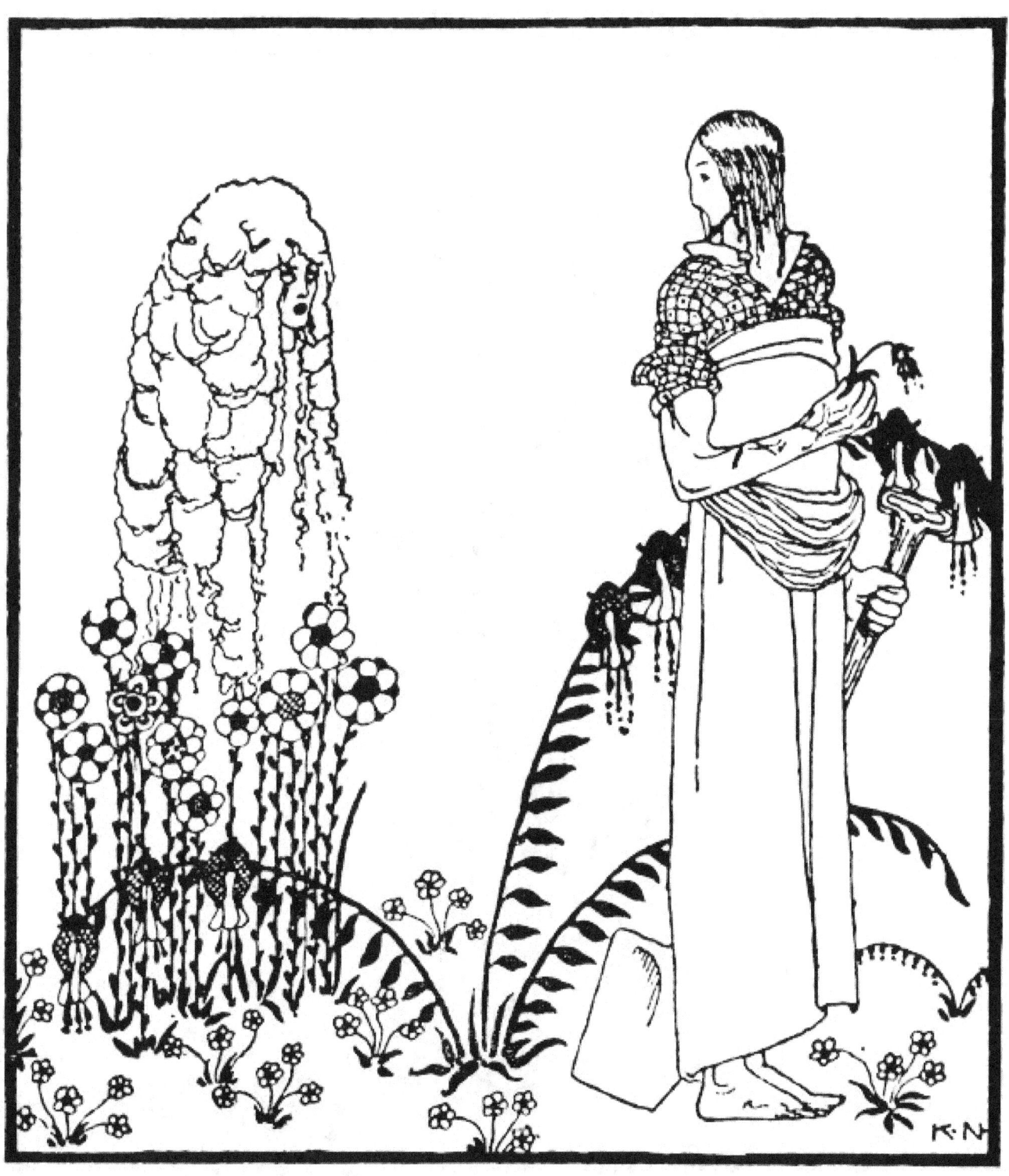

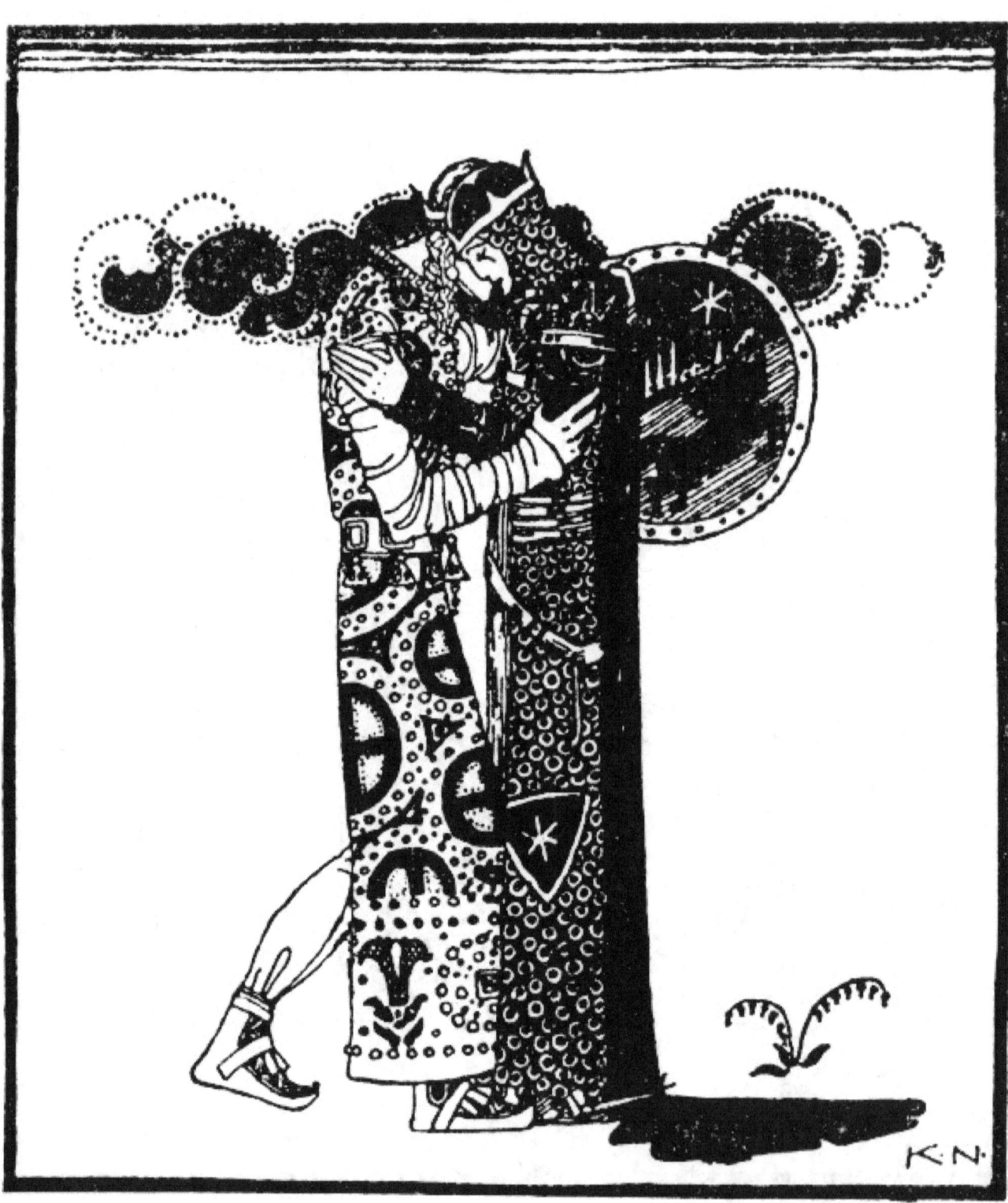

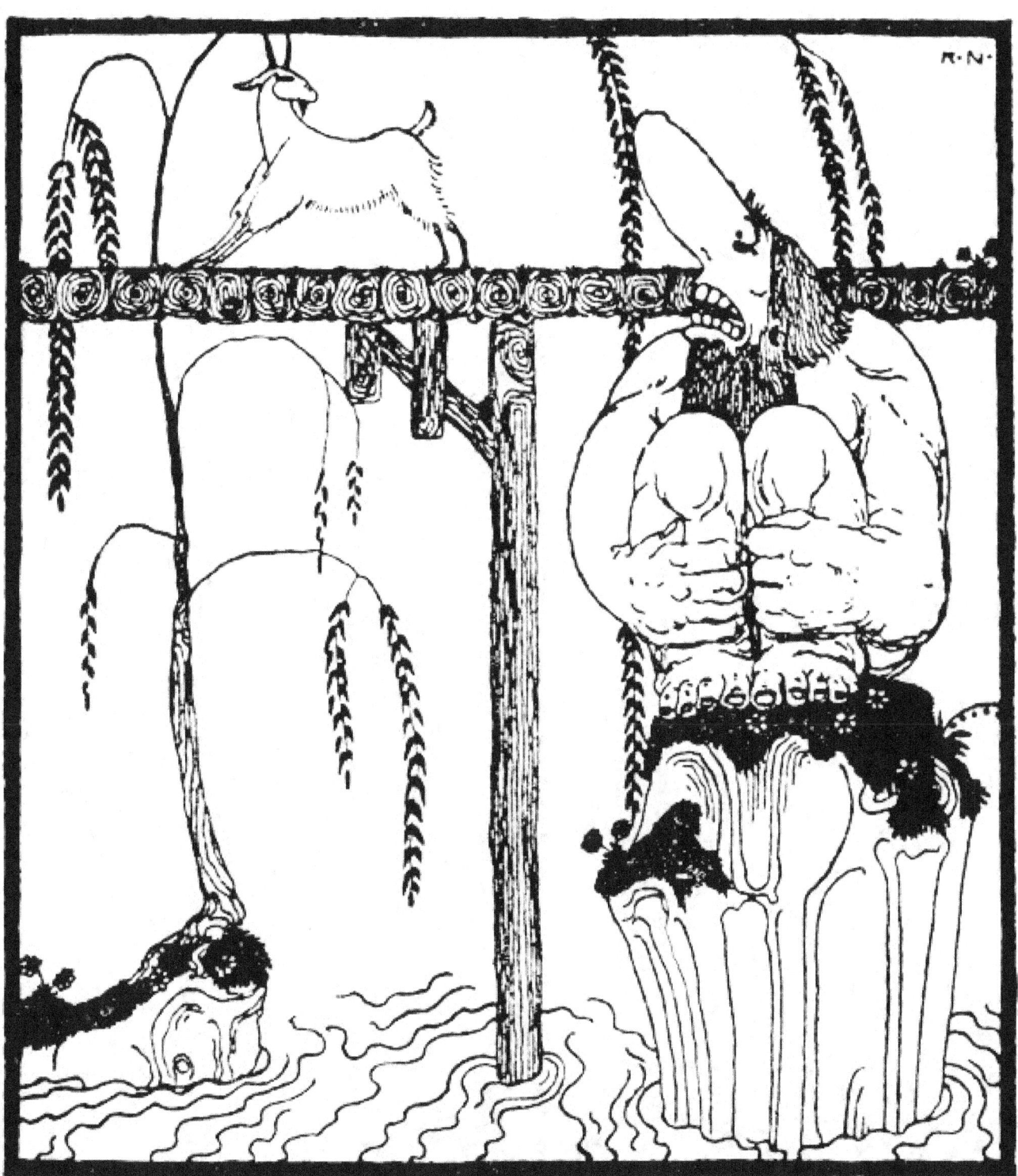

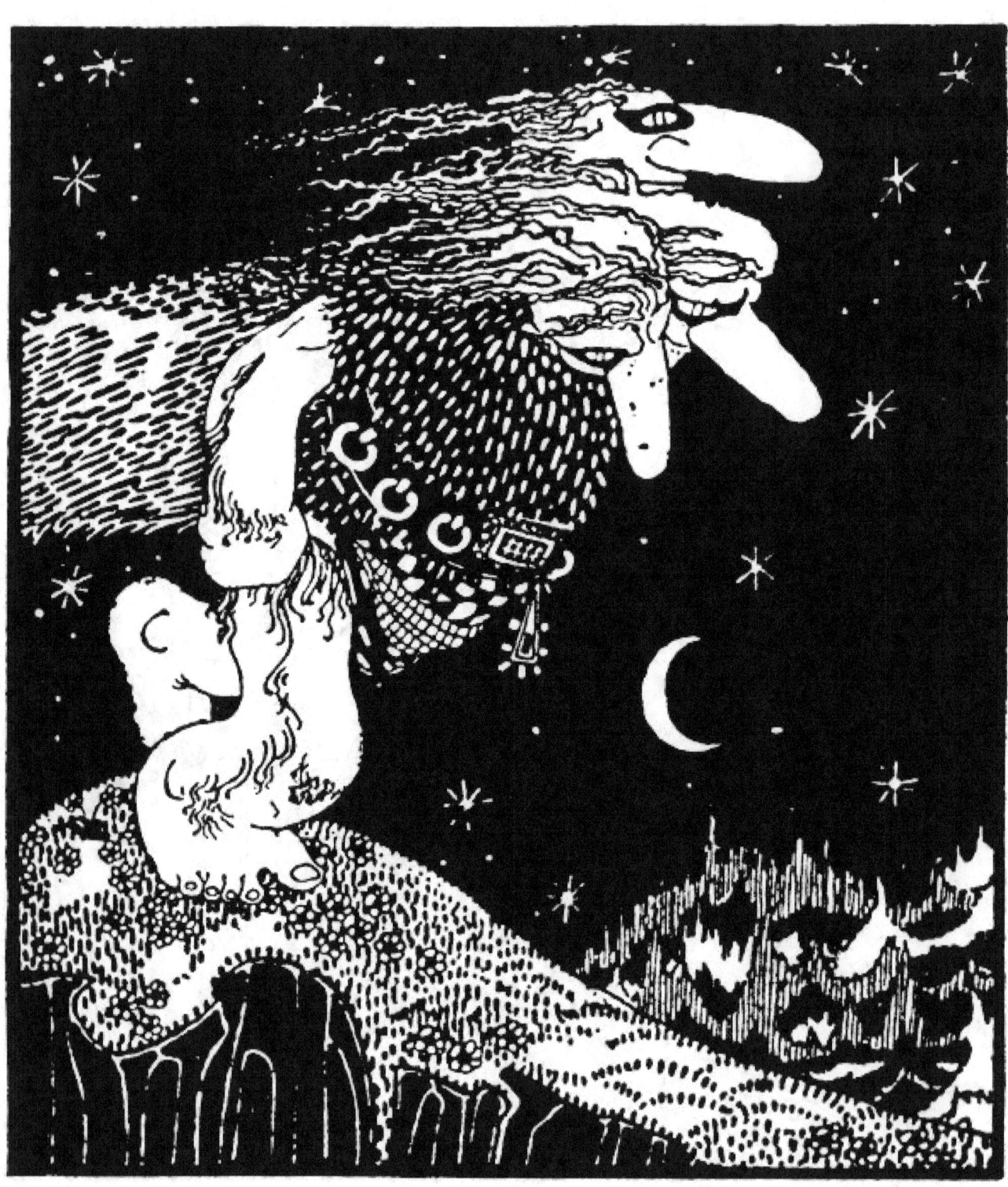

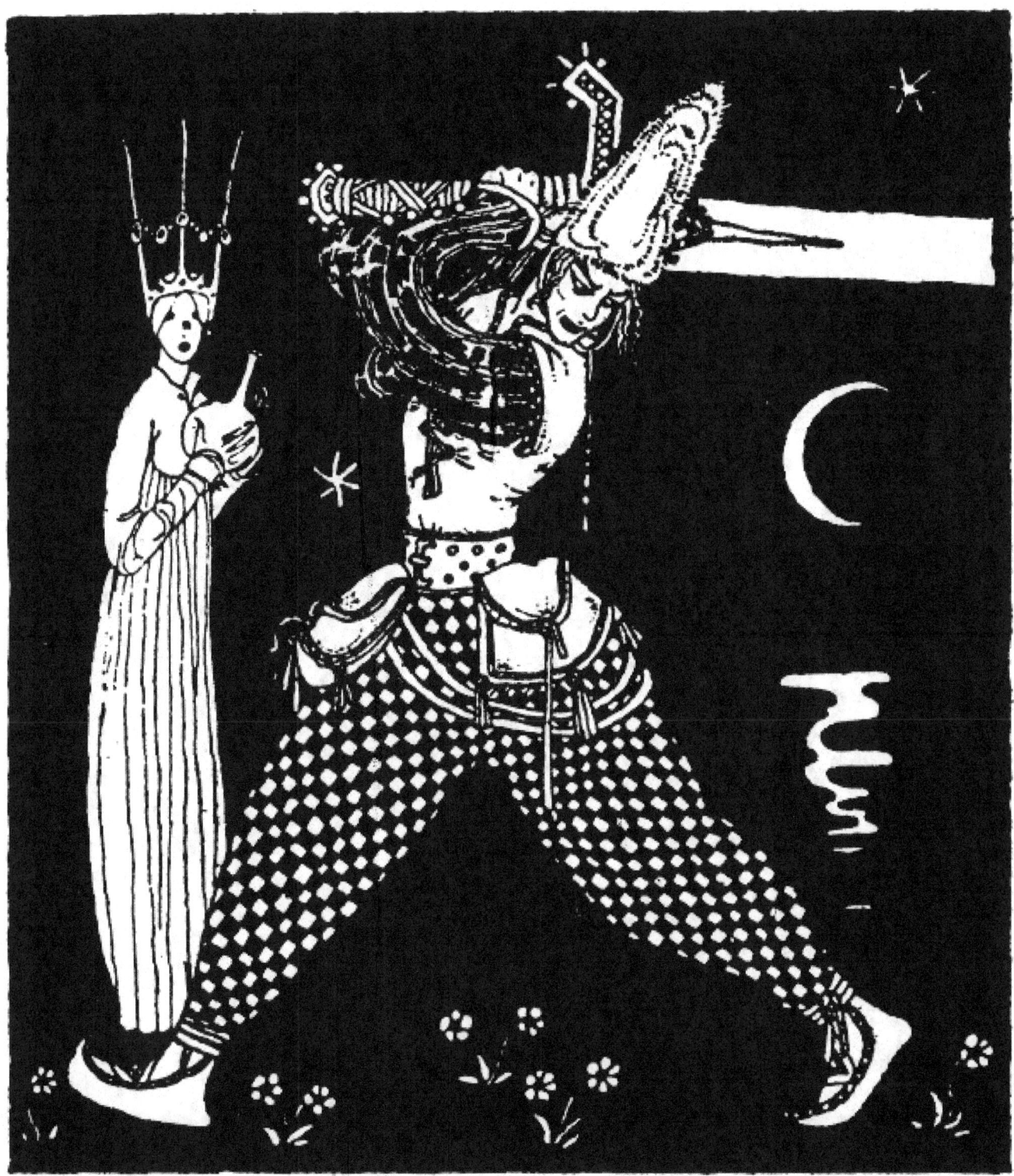

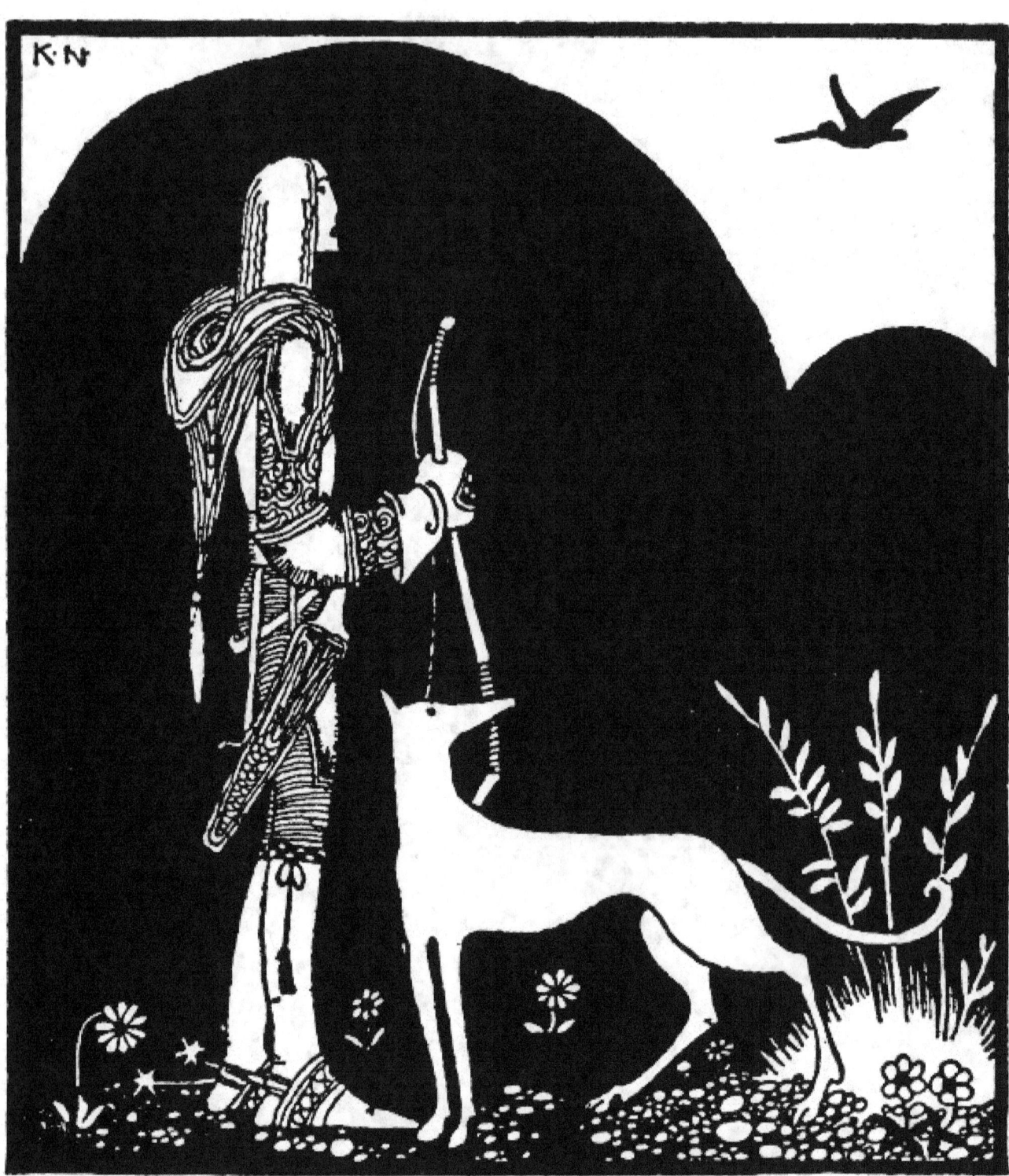

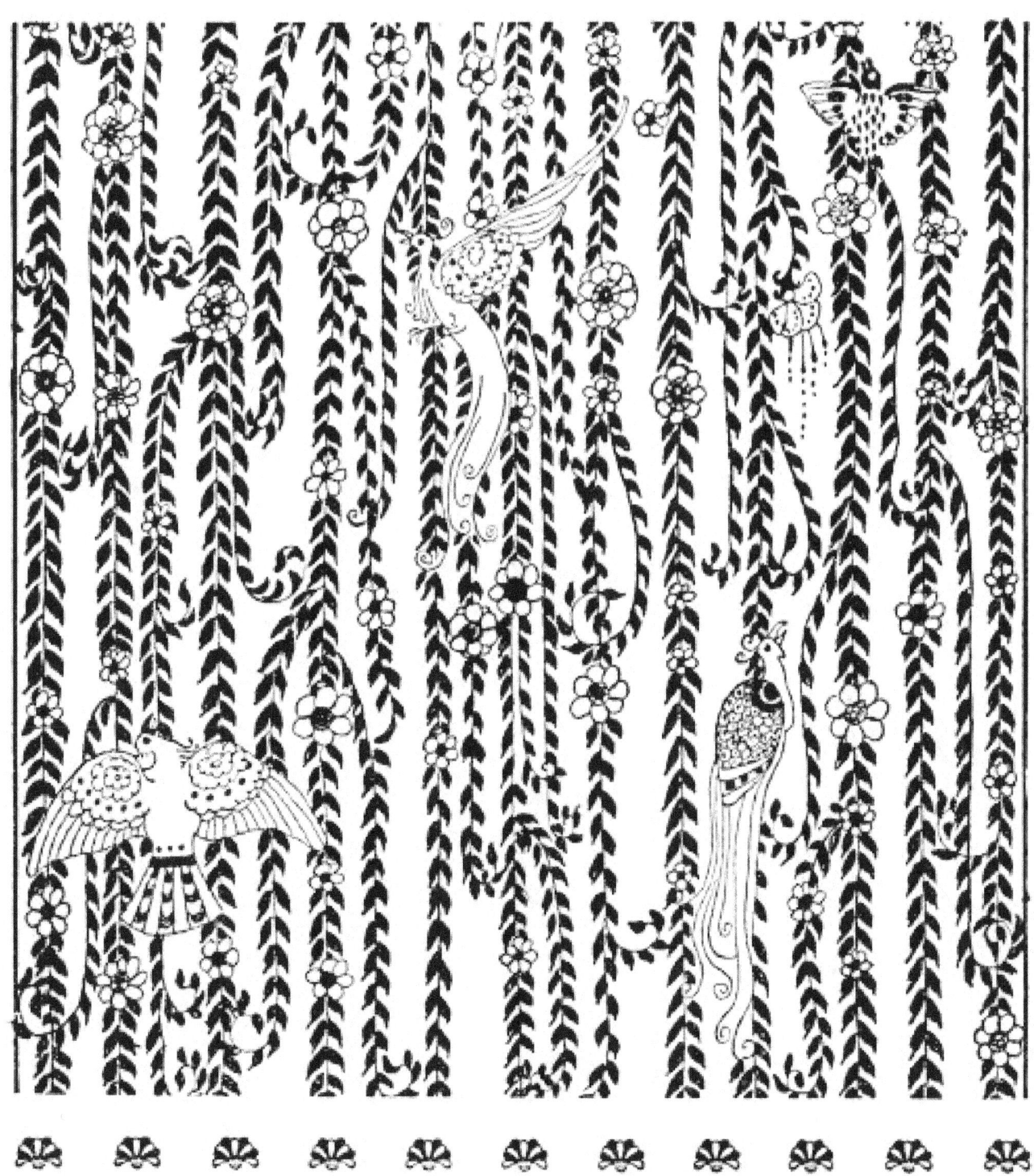

Tom Vroman

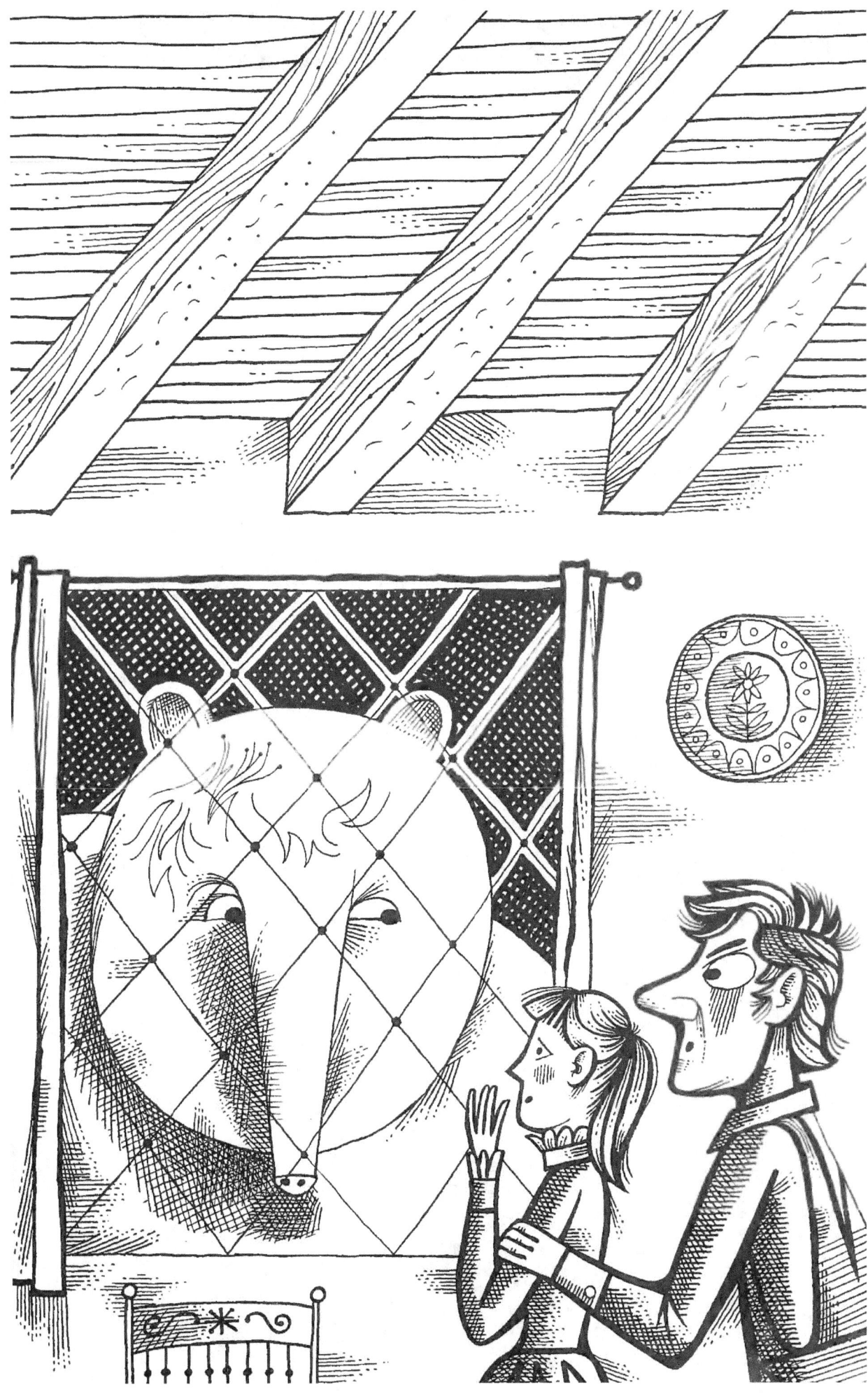

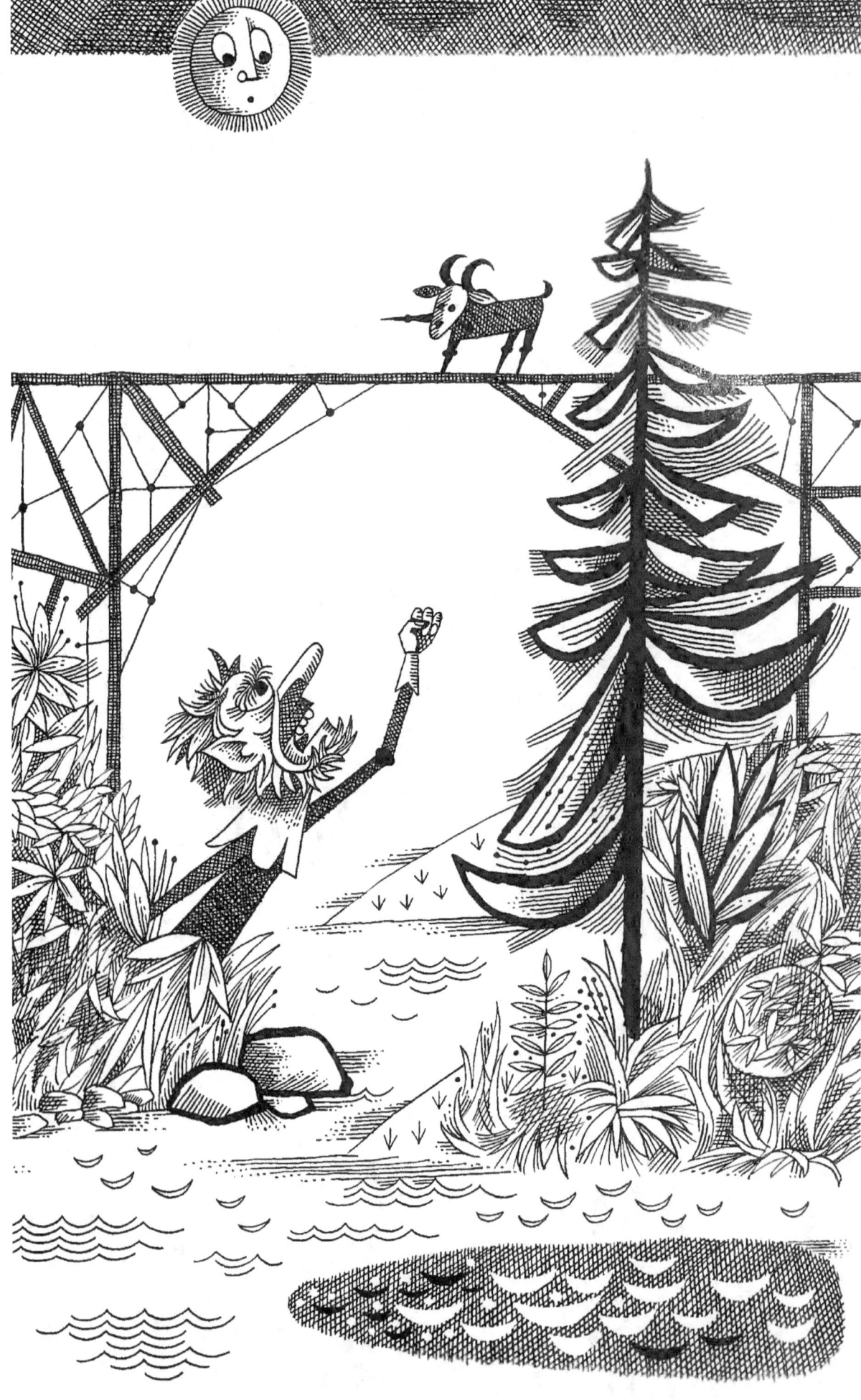

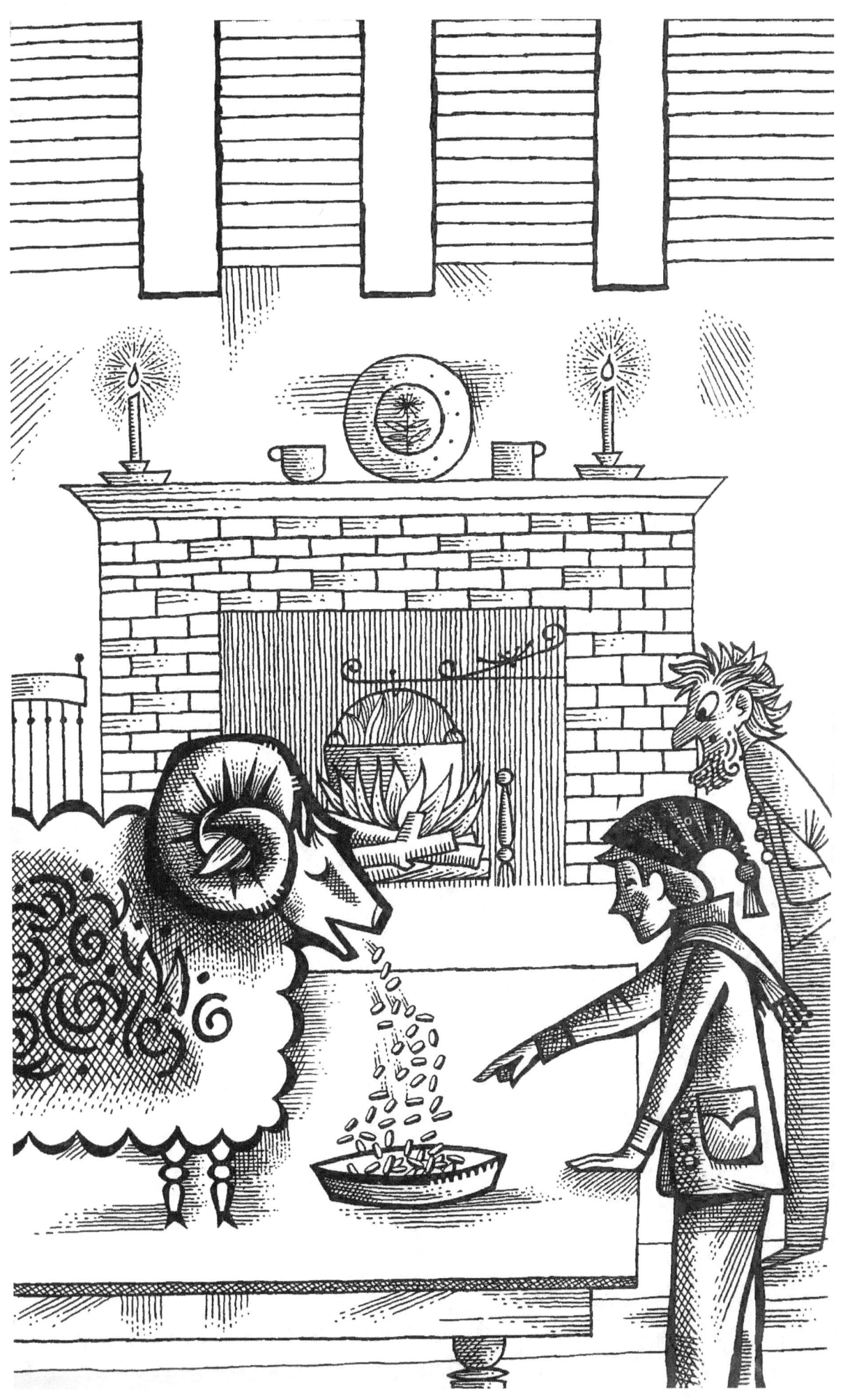

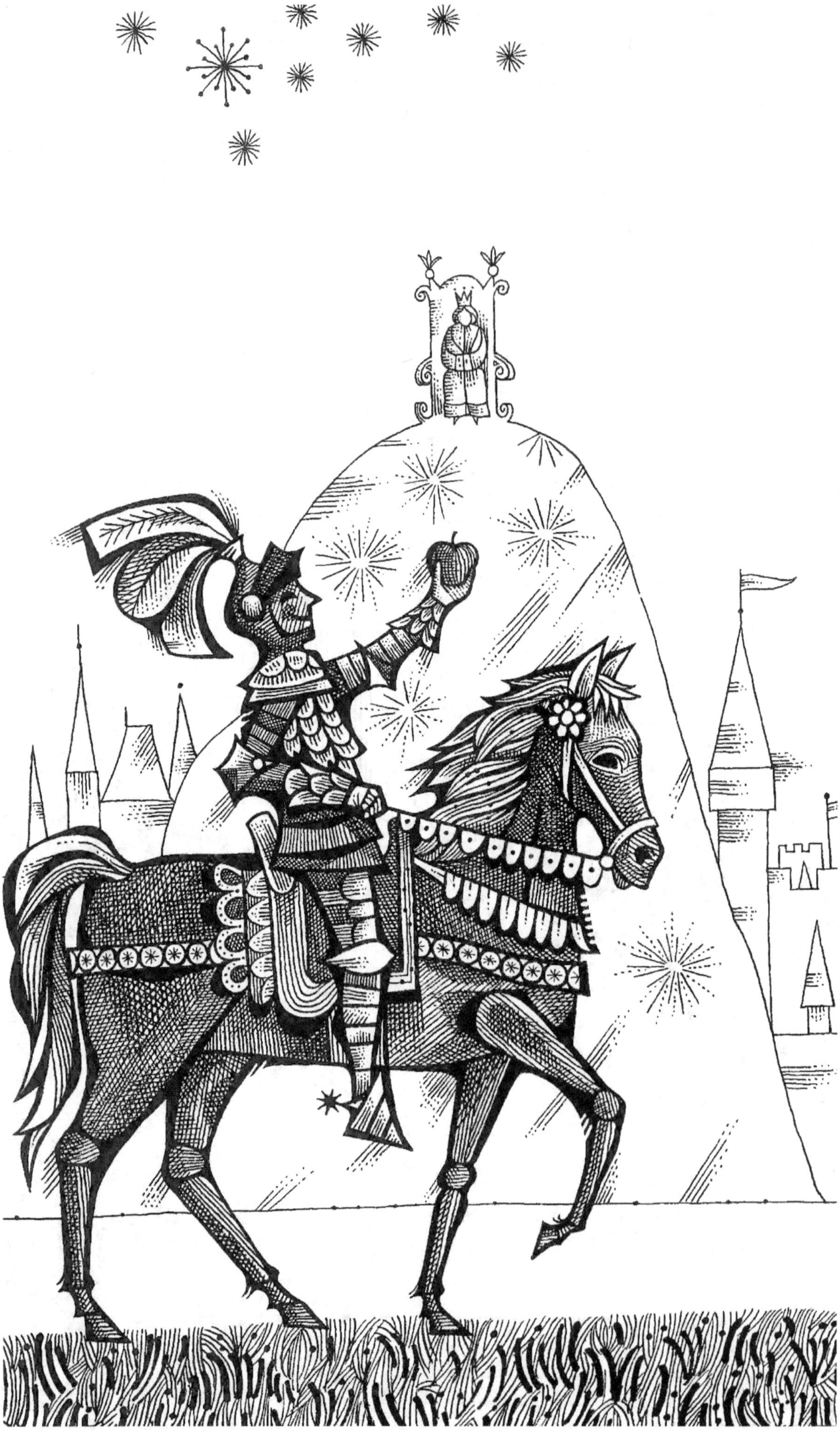

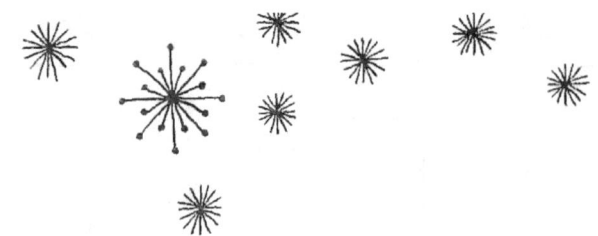

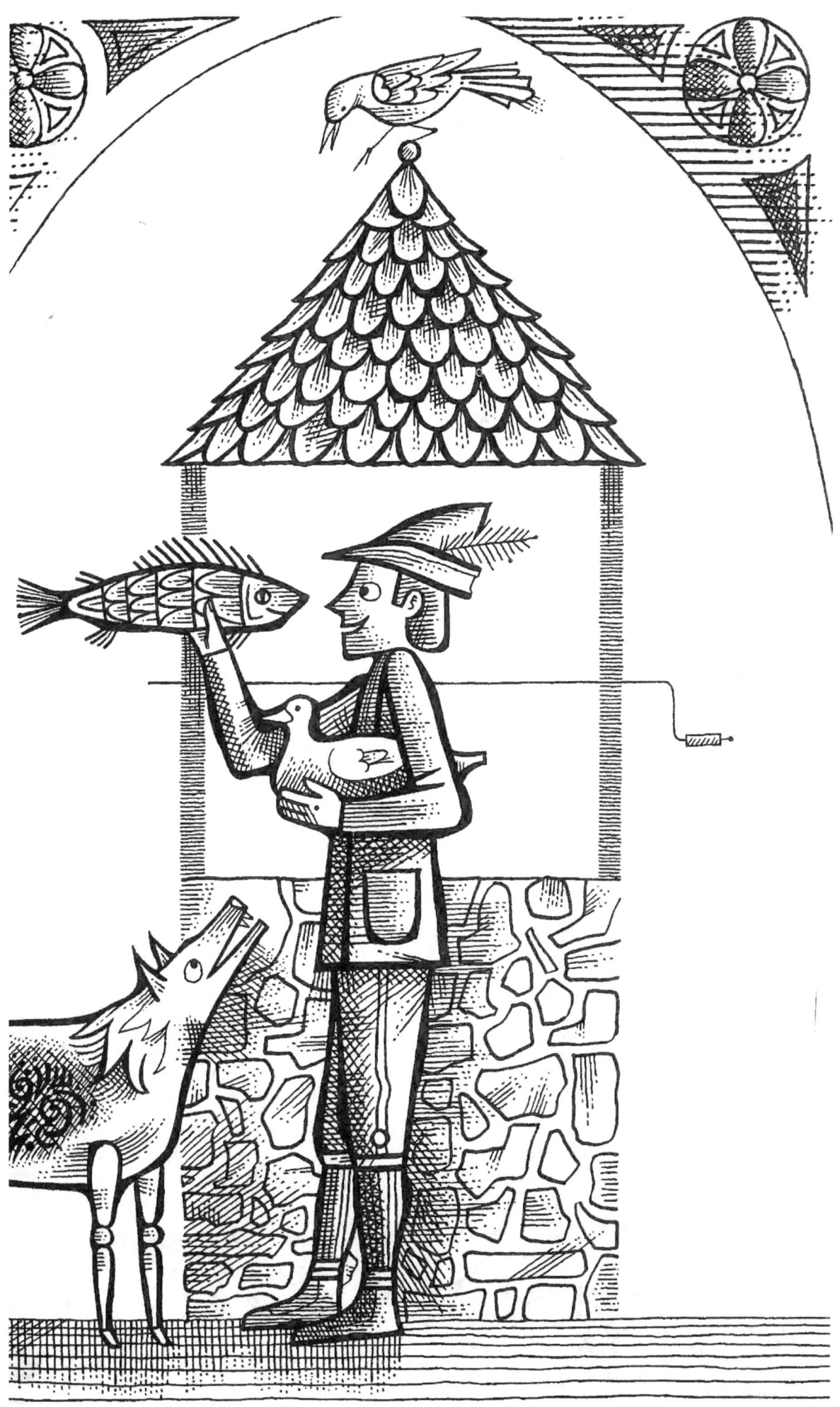

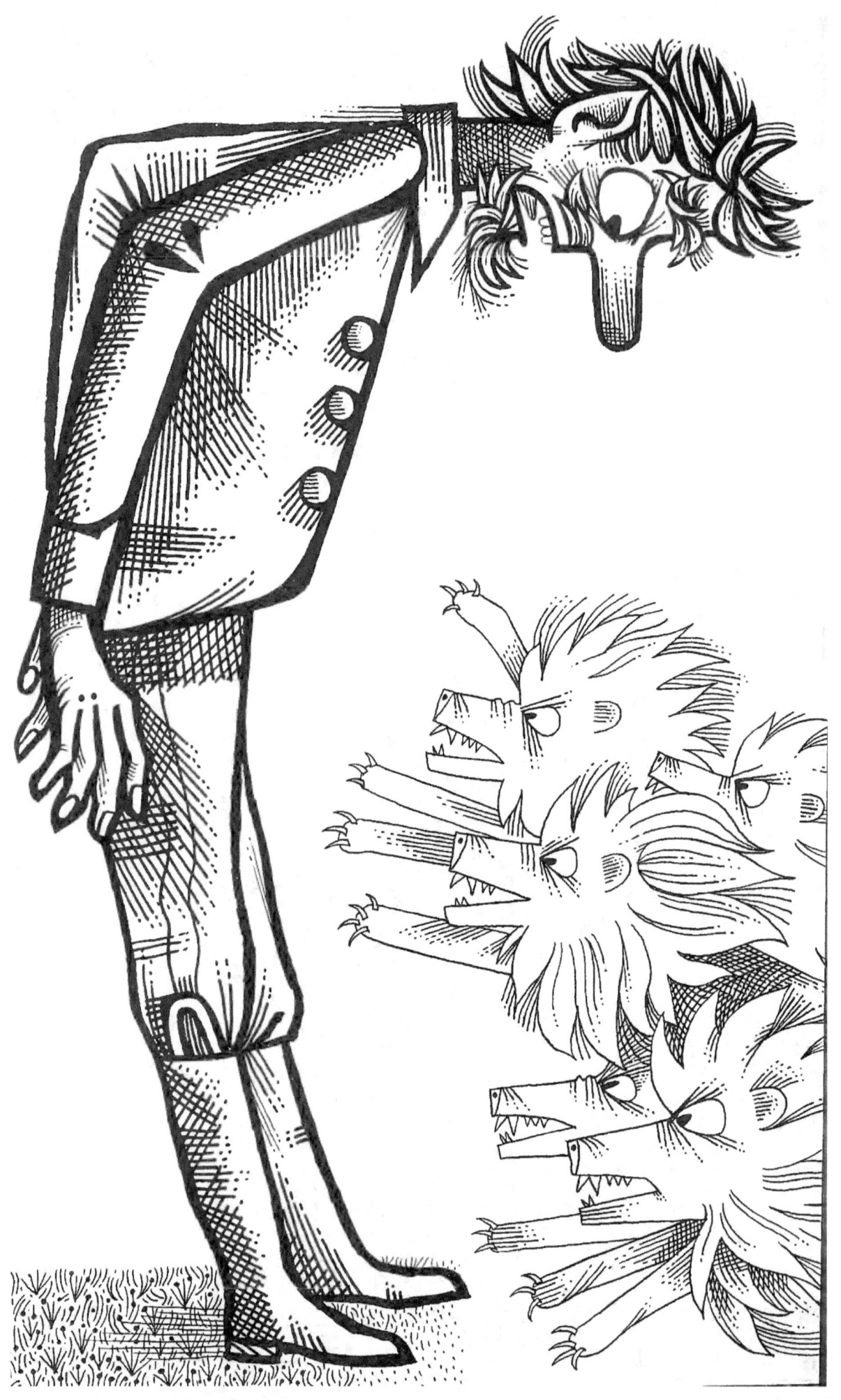

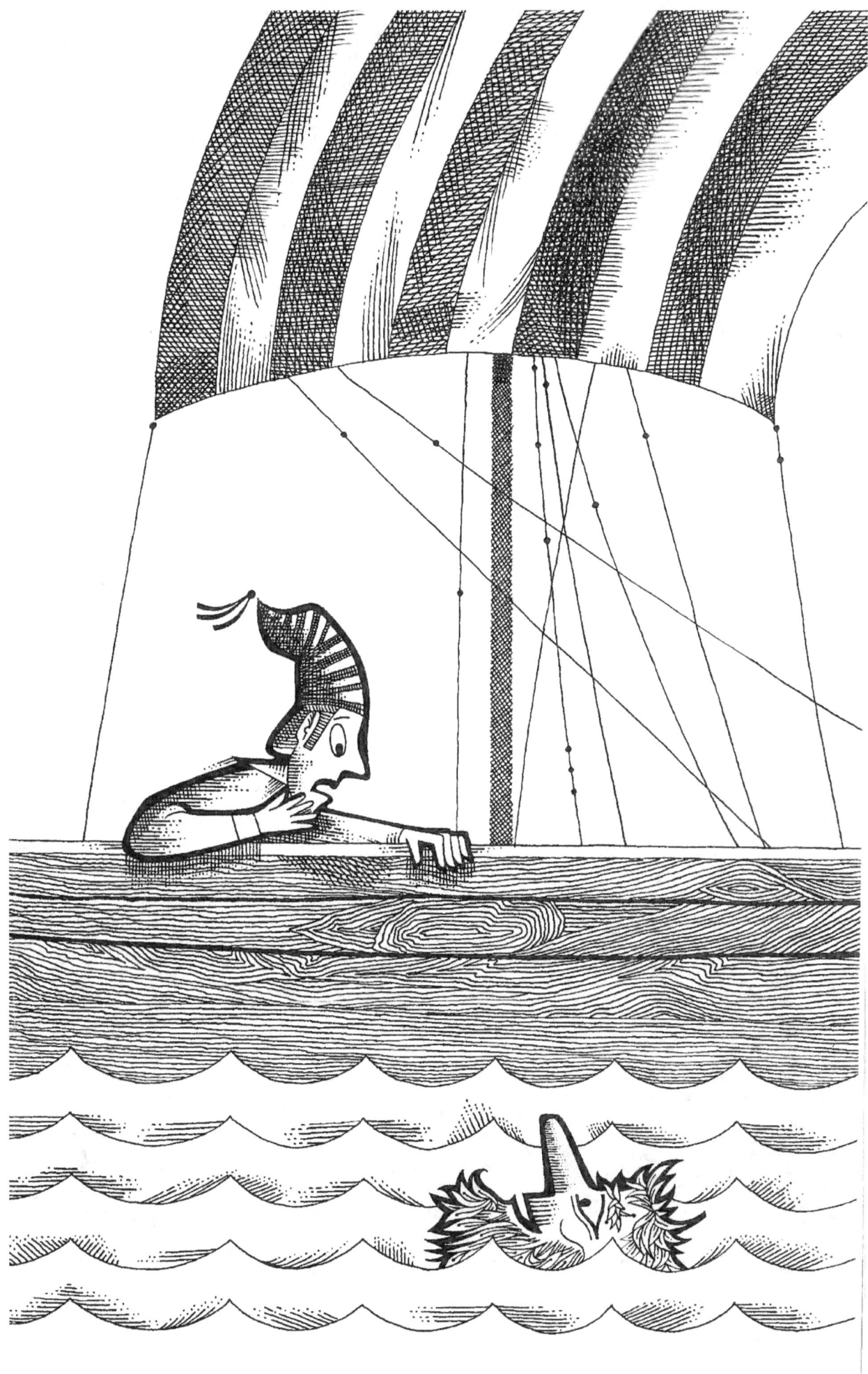

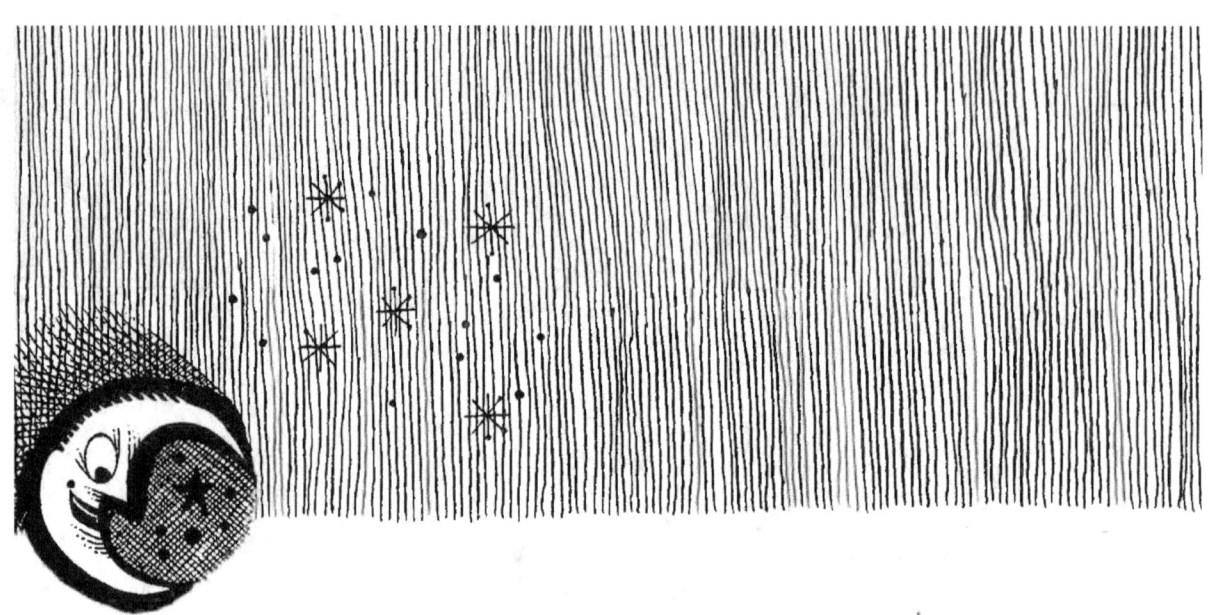

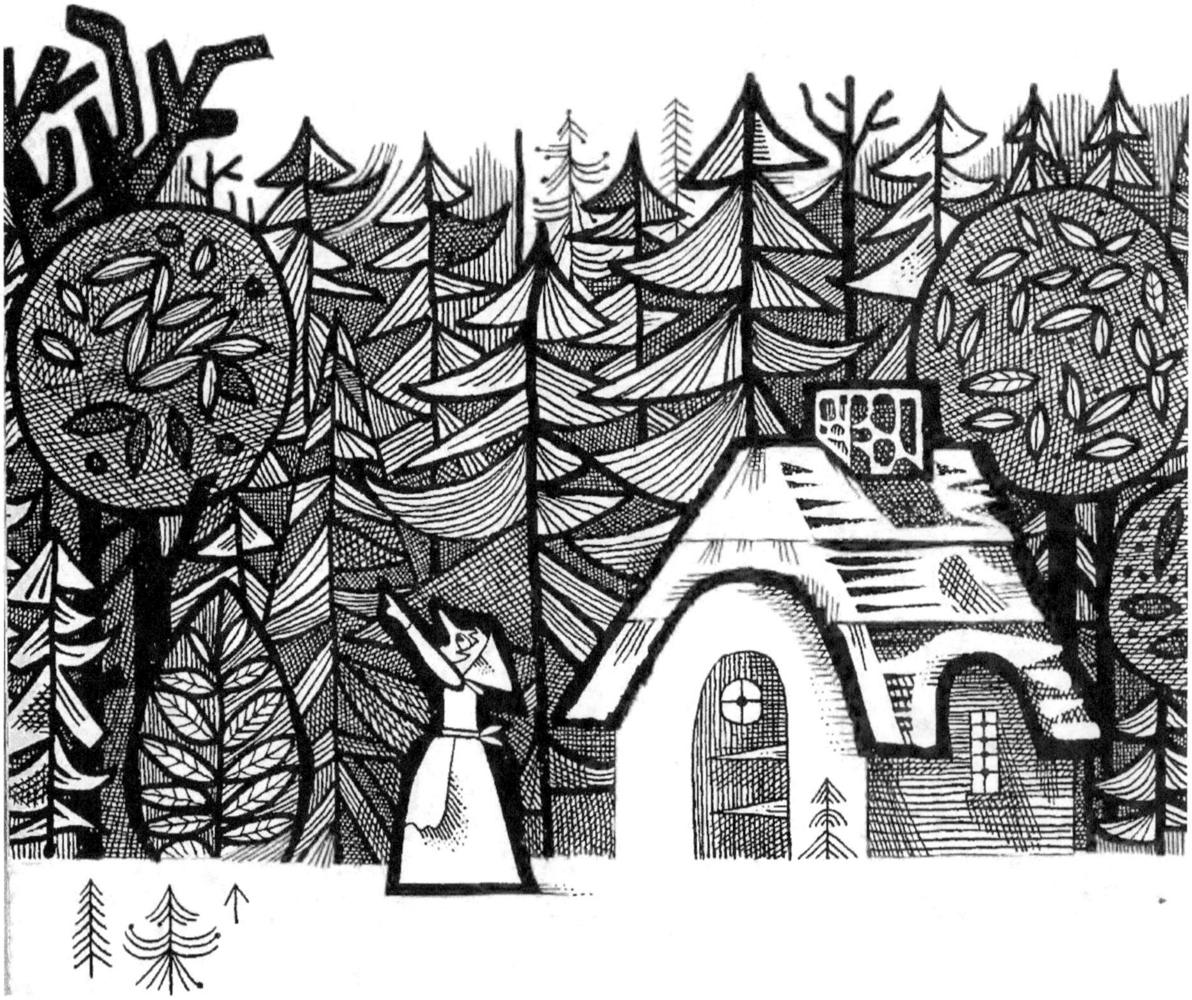

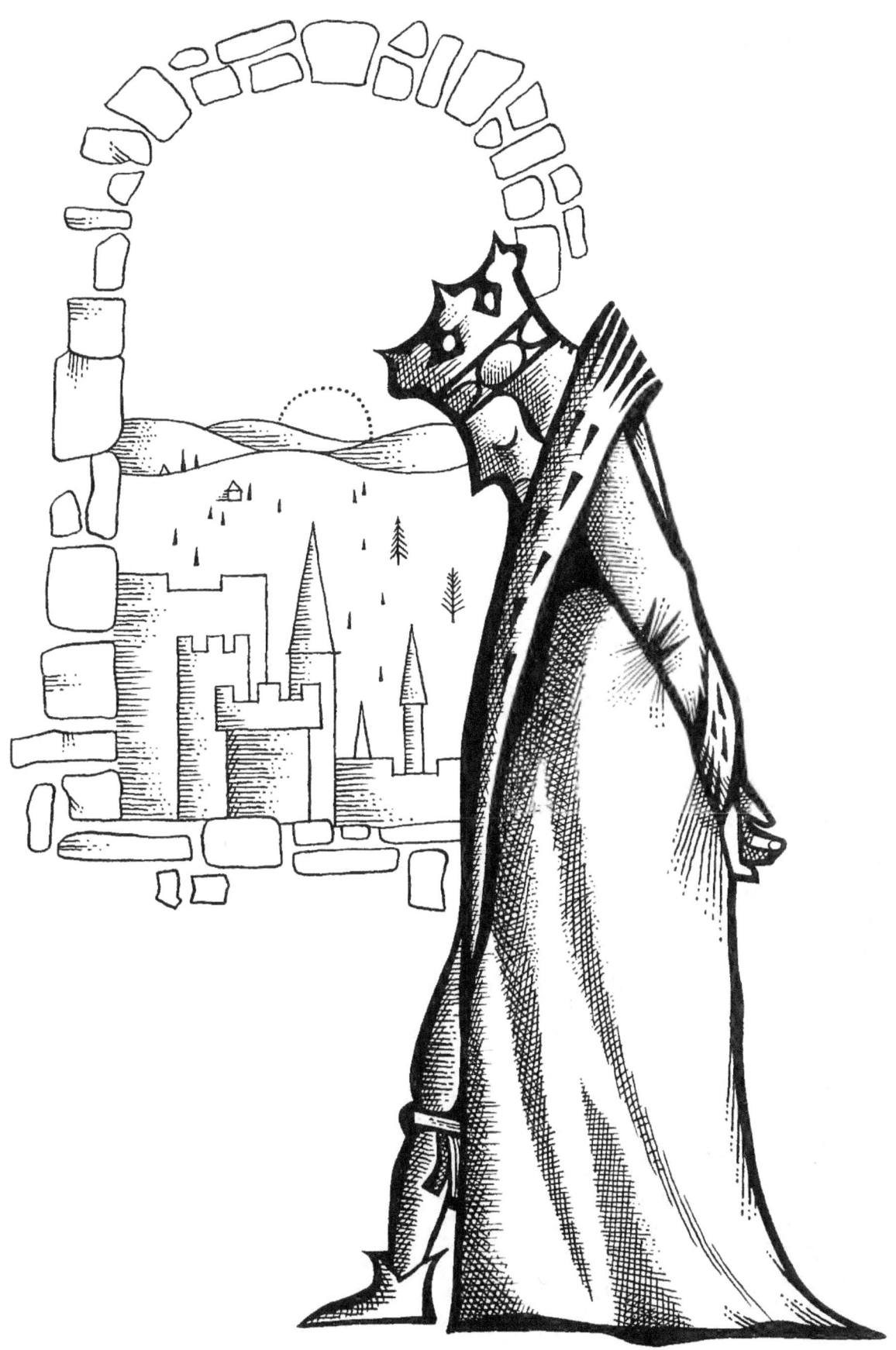

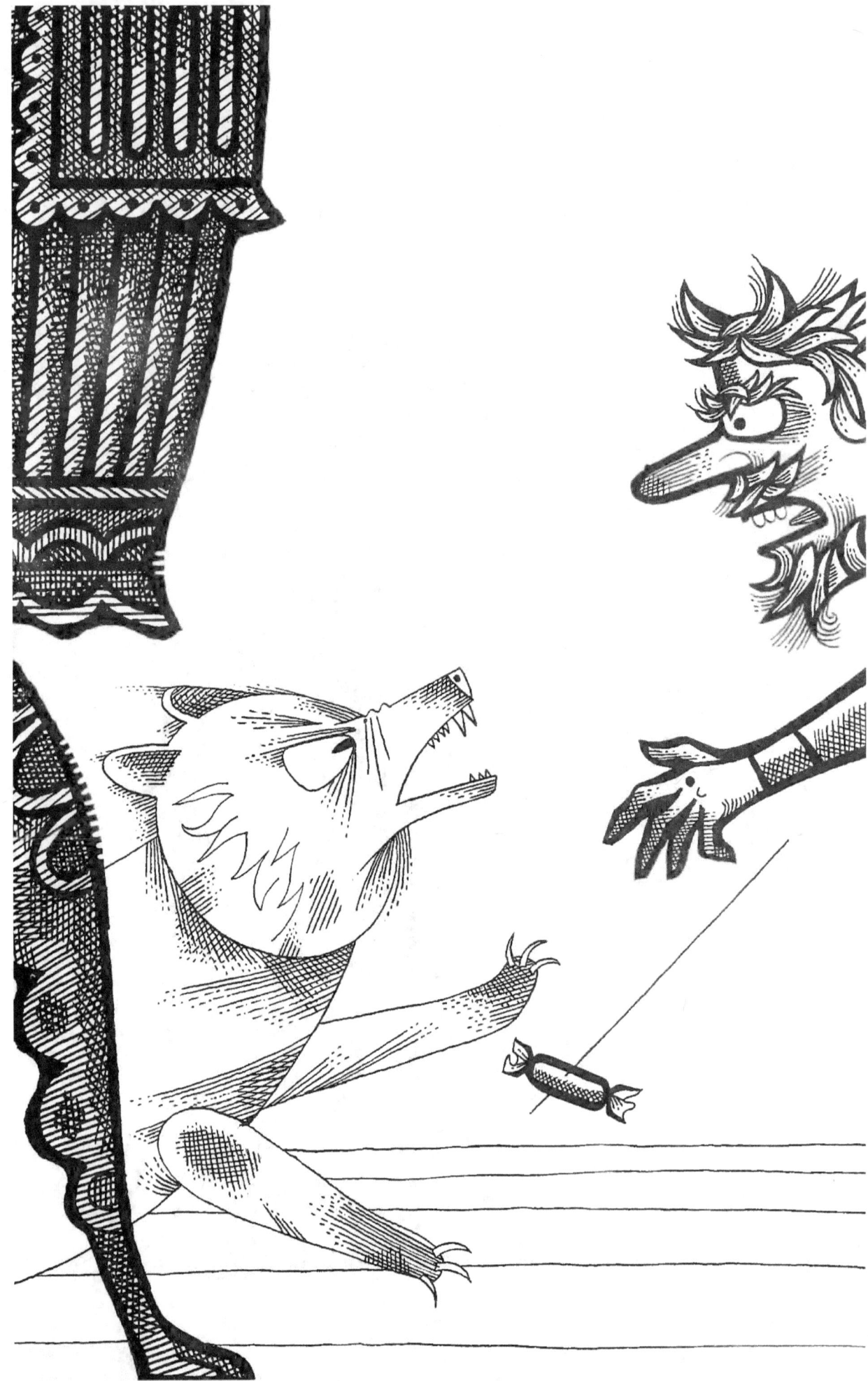

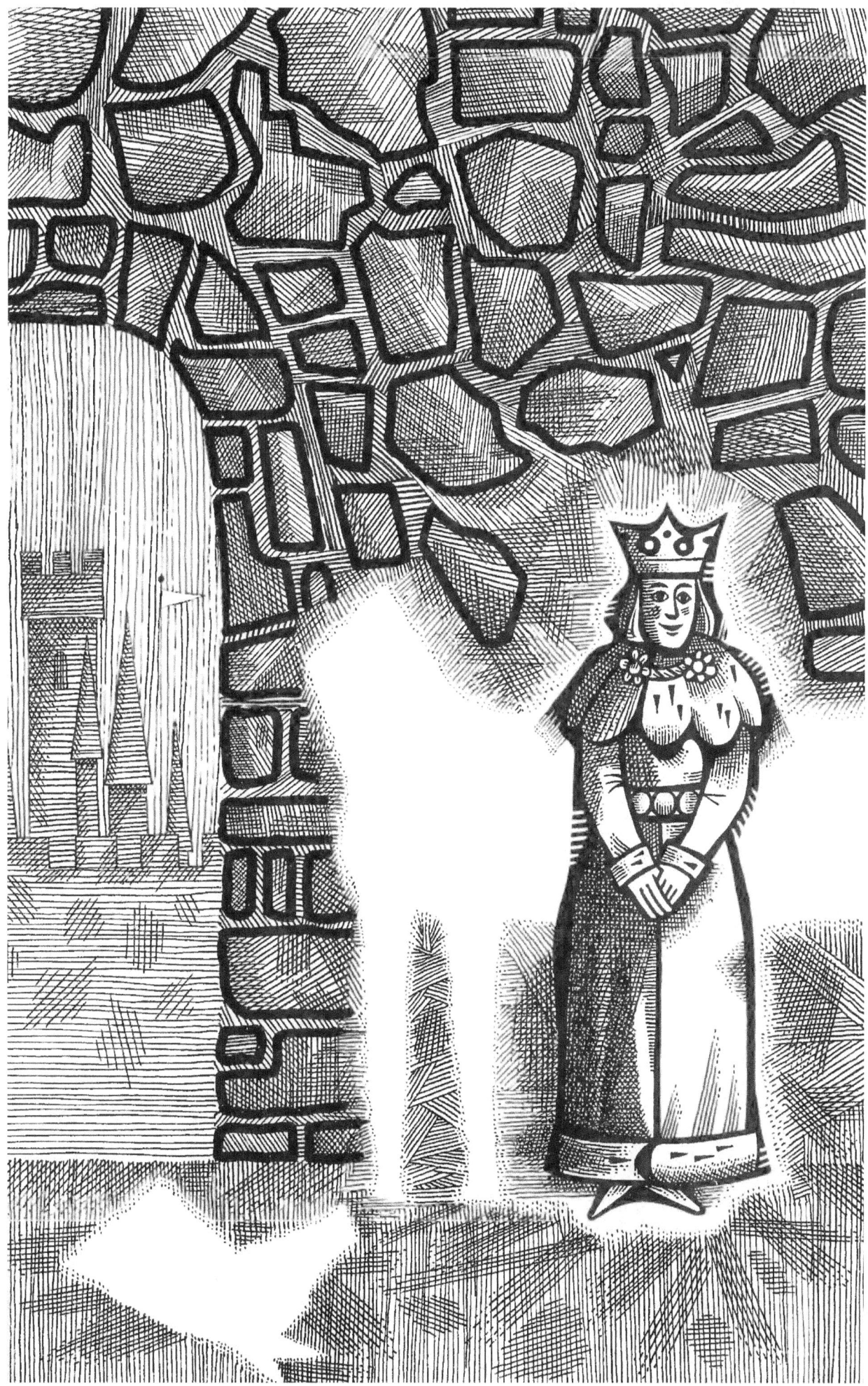

www.ingramcontent.com/pod-product-compliance
Lightning Source LLC
Chambersburg PA
CBHW082222220526
45470CB00010B/3277